# 365 DAYS OF HAPPINESS

## Peris DeVohn Edwards

*"The measure of the moral worth of a man is his happiness. The better the man, the more happiness. Happiness is the synonym of well-being"*

*- Bruce Lee*

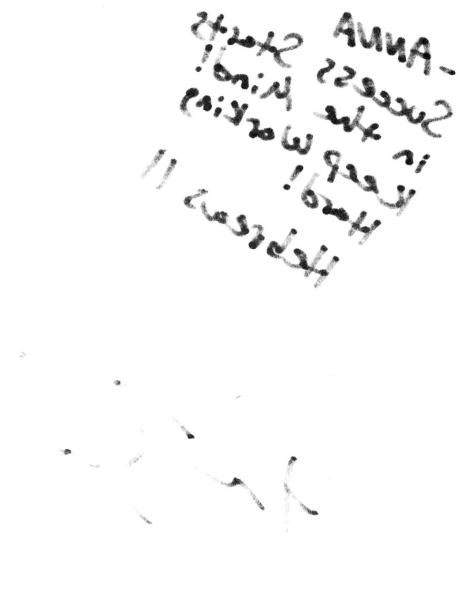

**<u>Book Dedication:</u> Auntie Tonya Daniels-Wilson**

*This, being my first book to be published, means that it's very special to me; it's my baby. I'm blessed to have a lot of great people in my life who believe in me and inspire me to do better, but I would specifically like to dedicate this book to my Auntie Tonya Daniels-Wilson.*

*Thank you so much for being a light to so many people with the time that you spent on this earth. Some things we all knew about you is that you were going to show your praise and love for Christ, speak your mind, cheer for the Dallas Cowboys, and love and care for others unconditionally. One of the last conversations we had, you specifically told me, "You need to find a wife, Nephew. A man that finds a wife finds a good thing and you need to hurry up and finish writing your book so you can write mine; I have a story to tell too, Nephew".*

*Your words gave me the inspiration and discipline to finish this book, thank you so much. We all love and miss you very much but the Lord needed you back home. May you rest easy in heaven and watch over us all.*

*Love you. Your nephew, Peris.*

*Tonya Daniels-Wilson "Lisa"*
*Sunrise: September 6, 1970 Sunset: June 16, 2015*

# FOREWORD

"What do you want to do when you grow up?"

When I first met Peris Edwards (a student in high school, placed by cosmic blessing in my Senior English class), I asked him this very question and he told me he wanted to play in the NFL. Even though he was a phenomenal player, well-known in our school for his gifts and abilities on the field, I was no stranger to teenage boys telling me they intended to play in the (**name any national sport here**).

"Okay," I said. "What else?"

He looked confused. "What do you mean 'what else'?" He asked me.

I shrugged. "What is Plan B? What if the NFL doesn't happen? The best thing you can do for yourself is to always think of a Plan B before you need it." Having had this conversation with hundreds of boys before him, I was feeling pretty smart and wise in my stance.

Peris looked at me with a knowing smile and didn't hesitate in his response. "No, Mrs. Peters. The NFL *is* Plan B. My education is Plan A. You asked me what I wanted to DO, not who I wanted to BE."

Boom.

Mic Drop, as the kids say.

I can still remember feeling the tiny hairs on my arm stand up as I stopped handing out papers and stared at him. His words had struck a chord in me so powerful that I was literally dumbfounded. I wasn't prepared for the level of self-awareness his answer had shown and I had never before had a student who so effortlessly could differentiate between the musings of heart and brain. I didn't know yet, you see, with whom I was dealing. I certainly had no idea, in that moment, that ten years later, his words will still be teaching ME lessons.

What you see is what you get with Peris Edwards. He doesn't have to prove himself to anybody because, just as he knew of himself a decade earlier, **WHO HE IS** promotes itself. Truth, you see, is the easiest thing to sell. People crave it. Often, they'll pay any price for it – with their time, energy, emotions, and heart. The stories of this book are a compilation of that same self-reflection and same high level of self-awareness that I first witnessed in the author at the young age of 17.

The words you are about to read come from a place of sincere desire within Peris to do something, give more, *be better*. They will ignite a passionate flame within you, so powerful that the urge to fix your own shortcomings will suffocate your spirit into action. His words are inspiring; his message is Holy.

"What do you want to do when you grow up?"

I want to be like Peris Edwards. In the words of Mr. Edwards himself, "I want become more, so I can give more."

The student has become the teacher.

*--Katie Peters*

## Who Are You?

## God

## Deciding to Be Great

## What Do You Want?

## Commitment

## The Process

## Your Purpose

## Giving

## Don't Quit, Face Your Fears

## Dream Big

## The Prize

# HAPPINESS

Happiness: (noun) - the quality or state of being happy. Good fortune; pleasure; contentment; joy.

Happiness is a noun, meaning it can be a person, place, or thing and the choice is yours. The key word here is "choice." We have the power to wake up and choose every single day what or who we want to be happy about. The power to choose to be happy, to choose our thoughts, and how to use our time are the best powers we have. Happiness, success, and greatness are all synonyms for me and they're all choices we have to make on a daily basis.

Let's be honest, we all have blessings and we all have problems in this world, but whichever one we choose to focus more on will determine how much we will enjoy life. No one is exempt from adversities or struggles in life; that isn't a bad thing because it makes us uncomfortable which then forces us to grow stronger allowing us to be more thankful for the blessings we receive.

This is not a book for you to read and "become" happy, I hope that's not what you're looking for. No book, nor can anyone else, make that decision for you except you. I'm here to tell you through personal experience that happiness, joy, greatness, and success all come from within; it all starts with attitude and perspective, not your situation. I think to be happy one must do a few things: love yourself, love God, love others, serve others, find a purpose and live it. None of these things are outside of you and that is the most important part to remember because we'll often chase happiness in the form of accomplishments, money, success, or seeking others love or approval to feel worthy.

My goal for you after reading this book is for you to realize that you possess everything that you need to get you to where you need to go. Doubt, fear, negativity are all distractions to keep you from believing that you have the power. All you need is faith in God and yourself and you can do whatever it is that your heart desires.

Happiness for me is spreading happiness to you and encouraging others to find and live their purpose in life despite the odds and the fear we all have in some shape or form. Once and only when we decide what we're going to do, then and only then will everything start to work in our favor by God's grace; but it all starts with you. Success and happiness can only be defined by you for your own life. Thank you for purchasing my book and I pray that it helps you and that you will be blessed beyond measure in whatever it is that you decide to do. God bless.

"People are as happy as they make their mind up to be"

- Abraham Lincoln

# THE INSPIRATION

*"There can never be success without happiness,
and no man can be happy without dispensing
happiness to others"*

*- Napoleon Hill*

I nspiration is a big deal to me and always has been. The word "inspire" originates from the Latin word "inspirer" meaning to breathe upon or into. To inspire someone, I think is the greatest gift God put in all of us. The most beautiful thing about being able to inspire is that God puts something in all of us to inspire in different ways; even if it's inspiration for the same purpose, it's in a unique way coming from each individual. Whether it's consciously or subconsciously, we are all inspiring and being inspired at all times.

One thing we do need to be conscious of is that we are inspiring in a positive way. Tony Dungy, one of my favorite authors and people, said, "We all are leaders but where are you leading people?" That is a great question, because whether we like it or not or know it or not, someone is watching us and inspiring to be like us, rather that's in a positive or negative way.

With my faith and religion being Christianity, someone once said to me, "You may be the only bible someone ever reads." Before I respond to that quote, I want to mention something else that I once posted as a Facebook status. "One thing I've observed is that when you only talk religiously, you mostly will only reach and inspire religious people. I can only speak for myself but I don't only want to limit myself to inspire Christians just because that's my religion and beliefs. I want to inspire and help EVERY ONE of all mankind and beliefs or having none at all. I'm no one to judge you for your choice of life; long as it's positive and it betters you and doesn't violate the rights of others, then I am all for it. We can agree to disagree on everything else but still better the world together."

I'm a Christian, an unapologetic one at that, and VERY proud of it. I also know to change the world I have to get down in it and at the same time, try not to be of it. Just because I'm surrounded by things and people who are not like me, that does not, and will not, put my beliefs or spirituality at risk because I know who I am and I'm 100% confident in that. I know I have to be very conscious of how I try to inspire people; I have to meet people where they are, it's not about me and I cannot expect people to see things how I do. It's my job as a Christian, and just a human being in general, to love people anyway; religion is not meant to divide people just because you don't agree on it. There is no way I can expect to inspire as many people as possible if I think and act as if what works for me is the only way.

I wanted to say that to make my audience aware that I don't believe my beliefs are superior to the next, I'm all for anything that's positive that makes you a better person and betters the world as a whole. This book is to inspire you to be a better you, if that happens to be Christianity, then I would be very happy. If it's another religion, I'm just as happy. If it's not religion at all and you're just inspired to become a better you, then I am still happy. This book is not a way to convert anyone into anything besides being a better you and bringing out of you what your heart truly desires, nothing more nothing less. Christianity is not only a part of who I am but it made me who I am today, so it's inevitable this book will have Christianity as a main focus point because I would not be giving you the real me if it wasn't a part of this book.

Back to the statement someone said to me, "you may be the only bible someone ever reads." After hearing that and digesting what it actually meant, I decided that it could be taken metaphorically or literally after pondering over it.

# I'M A CHRISTIAN

*"Occasionally we talk about our Christianity as something that solves problems, and there is a sense in which it does. Long before it does so, however, it increases by the number and the intensity of the problems. Even our intellectual questions are increased by the acceptance of a strong religious faith... If a man wishes to avoid the disturbing effect of paradoxes, the best advice is for him to leave the Christian faith alone"*

*- Elton Trueblood*

Let's say, for example, a friend, co-worker, or a family member is either a non-believer or thinking about becoming a believer and they're on the edge and liable to go in either direction, this is a crucial and delicate time with anyone with anything. Not just with religion, believing in something or someone that's new or different is a scary thing; change is hard but the only thing constant in life is change. They might not be at the point in their spiritual faith to constantly go to church, pray, pay tithes, study the bible, and most importantly keep their relationship strong with God, because we'll just say they aren't there yet. This could be due to various reasons: they didn't grow up in a house that believed in God, maybe they did and became rebellious, or they may just flat out not be interested once they became of mature age to make their own decisions.

Whatever the reason may be, that's neither here nor there and it really doesn't matter. I, myself, being a believer and a child of God may be the closest that someone like this will ever get to reading a bible; simply by observing me and my lifestyle as a believer. This is speaking for both types of non-believers, the one who has no interest in the religion whatsoever and the ones who are interested but don't know how to go about finding religion so they just sit back and observe the believers.

Picking up the Holy Bible and reading it can be very discouraging for many reasons, this goes for believers as well as non-believers. Things such as you may not know where to start, can't break down the word usage, you don't feel mature enough in Christianity yet, or it could be other reasons. These are all things I've struggled with and still do to this day, before and after accepting Christ at the age of 17. (I found it to be a lot easier for me personally to get a study Bible that has notes and breaks each scripture down.) So if a believer can struggle and be discouraged just imagine a non-believer on the edge of becoming or not, one small thing could sway them either way. It could be someone who claims to be a believer but not accurately representing Christianity to the best of their abilities (doesn't mean to be perfect), that's where the criticism starts and cannot really be argued unless with good reasoning. But like I always say, and will further elaborate on, it's the people that are flawed not the religion.

If you're discouraged to read the bible and study Christianity, or any faith you believe in, but you're interested consciously or subconsciously, what's the next best thing you can do? The answer is to study someone who "claims" to study the bible and live out their religion faithfully. (Not perfectly but faithfully, the distinction is vital.) Referring back to the quote that is them simply reading you as the only bible they'll ever read, if you're a good bible (metaphorically) to read then you will not be their last one. I keep saying if they're interested subconsciously or consciously because many times you may have tried to introduce them to God (I personally try to be VERY cautious of this unless they show a strong interest or at least some interest), but they weren't receptive or claimed to not be interested. Quite the contrary when a Christian or a person filled with the Holy Spirit and good energy is a living testimony of God and you're around that individual, you cannot help but become interested in why they are so joyful and fulfilled.

We all know that energy is transferred not destroyed. No different than when you talk to a baby in a happy voice, the baby laughs; you're just transferring energy, there's really no difference with adults. We are the same exact way, "birds of a feather flock together" is how the saying goes. When the Holy Spirit lives within you, it attracts people towards you more than wealth, money, cars, and success. But I cannot prove it through this book, just like I cannot prove faith; it's simply something you have to experience, words do little to no justice.

Faith is not based on facts; it cannot be proven or disproven, only experienced. If you claim to be a believer, a non-believer and/ or even sometimes believers, will always be watching you and how you live. So you can either be inspiring someone towards your religion and faith or inspiring them to stay away from it. Whether you like it or not, this is the responsibility that comes with being a child of God and accepting Jesus Christ as your Lord and savior and believing he died for your sins. In my opinion, Christianity or religion itself is just the one example that I'm using because I believe there is a responsibility that comes with EVERYTHING when you become a part of something that is bigger than yourself. That can be a sports team, family, fraternity, job, sorority, marriage, or anything else you can think of. To use a sports metaphor, the name on the front of your jersey (the team's name) is more important than the name on the back of your jersey (your last name), meaning the team is more important than the individual player. Team Christianity is no different from this example.

Before I go any further I want to make sure I'm clear on something, being a Christian doesn't mean you live perfect and you don't have bad times in life. No matter what you believe in, there's not one person who is immune to adversity. I want to humbly come before anyone and apologize "if" ever I presented or came off as a Christian man or human being in general as if I had no trials or tribulations or that I have life all figured out in any way, shape, or form. That is far from the truth and the upcoming pages in this book will reveal that, but I also know the truth is easily lost from the outside looking in or when there is a miscommunication.

I have much better questions than I have answers (that's why I love reading more than writing). I have negative thoughts and unfortunate things happen to me beyond my control. I am not exempt from life's ups and downs just because I am gifted with a blessing to be inspirational or because of my religion. One thing I do know, understand, and more importantly accept is that God's plan and understanding of my own life is bigger and better than that of my own. This allows me not to worry or dwell on too much; I've made the decision to be happy and God is the center of that. I will remain this way, nothing and no one will take that away.

My blessings far outweigh anything life will throw at me so I refuse to let the bad spoil the good and I refuse to focus on anything negative, period. It's no secret, that's it, I just have a little more faith than I have fear and doubt, meaning; *I have substance of things hoped for and evidence of things not seen Hebrews 11:1.* Once you make a decision to be happy or ambitious about anything, it will be tested. It will take a constant and conscious daily effort to keep and protect it; you'll never just "arrive" at this peak and stay there, you have to constantly get better every day with hard work to maintain and improve what you already have.

A Christian with his best efforts should remain humble when success or anything good happens. He may be glorified by the outside world because but they know any blessing is because of the good grace of God and he deserves all the praise. When the bad happens, a Christian doesn't blame God for their situations, they know that it's for a reason and that a lesson needs to be taken from it no matter how hard the storm may be; there is a message within it. A Christian should also know that during bad times this is a time to get closer to God because he's your only comfort and he will never put more on you than you can bear. Someone of faith doesn't pray to be out of the bad times, they simply pray for strength to endure them. Because they know that bad and good are just a part of life, they want to be well equipped rather than being unrealistic and trying to avoid hardships beyond their control. Then again, is it really bad if there's a lesson in it? *One shall not differentiate between good or bad, neither shall he make a substitute for it; and if he does substitute for it, then both it and the substitute shall be holy; it shall not be redeemed.* Leviticus 27:33

A Christian prays and thanks God in advance while in the storm for getting him out even though technically, he or she is still in it, physically, mentally, and emotionally. Yes, they are in the storm but not spiritually because the faith allows them to know that God will see them through whether they logically understand it or not. No matter what the world does to us negatively, it will always be overcome with the strength we receive from Christ. The spirit of a Christian should be in sync with the Most High; not of the world or your body because the flesh is weak, temporary, and cannot be satisfied or ever strong enough. The overall goal for a believer is to have such a great relationship with the Most High that no matter your situation, you can never tell if a Christian is doing good or bad as far as of this world. They always seem to be leveled off and at ease no matter the situation and that is the true happiness a non-believer should see. They may become curious and seek God because of you being that bible, learning that their situations don't define them.

The reality is that when you want good in life you can seek it out and when you want bad, you can seek that out too. Whether you're a believer or not, we as humans aren't good at balancing on our own, we tend to lean to one side. Unfortunately, the average person tends to think life is worse than what it actually is. Christianity is meant to be that balance that to an extent, you accept life for what it is and realize some things are beyond your control. You are more blessed than you realize so there's no need to complain much; be more thankful for your blessings because it's all perception.

Living as a good Bible to read also may make one who's already a believer curious and make them realize they're not where they need or want to be with their relationship with God. It may also make them feel as if they just need to get better because at the end of the day we all need to get better. Accepting Christ as your Lord and Savior is the easy part, you don't have to qualify for that because Jesus died for you to have that privilege; you now have to work at building a relationship with God, that's the challenge that never ends and it's never easy. No different from a wedding and the actual marriage. I've never been married but I know there's a difference so we all can be better and do better whether we are believers or not.

As I stated earlier, no one ever arrives, the journey is everlasting until you have no pulse; even in Christianity, it's a constant effort. We're motivated to get better and are inspired by others. We all have a job to inspire someone whether we acknowledge it or not. I'll say it again, religion has never been the problem, it's the people. Whether it's the people who claim to live by religion or the people who don't believe and bash the religion, promote what you believe and leave alone what you don't. If you don't believe in God or religion that's fine, do what you will but no need to be negative about religion as a whole or someone else's beliefs.

One thing I've come to observe is the difference between being pro something and anti-something. I'll use war as an example since religion is being exhausted in this chapter. If you're anti-war that means there needs to be war to practice anti-war. If you're pro-peace, then you simply don't want war to exist at all. Albert Einstein once said that "a country cannot simultaneously prepare for war and be pro-peace against war". So, if you don't agree or believe in religion then you don't need to go out of your way to be anti-religion just be pro whatever you believe in, for lack of better terms. I'm not saying that people who are ant-war don't want peace, but some people, they believe that war is necessary for peace, which I whole-heartedly disagree with, war only brings more war. If you prepare an army like Albert said then you'll continue to get exactly what you prepare for.

There's no need to waste time on something you don't believe in because that says more about you than whatever it is that you don't believe in. The responsibility that comes with religion or anything bigger than you is real and very important to realize because to whom much is given, much is expected and someone somewhere is waiting on you to mess up. This is not to say you have to live perfectly but you must live according to what you preach is all that I am saying. For example, if you're a prestigious coach and you coach a football team that's the "best" program, it's not that you're expected not to lose but you're expected when you do lose, to do it with class because it reflects the school, the coach, and the team. It's about the things you can control, not the things you can't when you're apart of something that's bigger than you.

To be a Christian doesn't mean you have an easier life at all, it's actually more difficult but at the same time it is better and always worth doing the Lord's work; better doesn't mean easier. They say nothing worth having comes easy, right? Again, I cannot say this enough, it's not that a Christian doesn't sin or their life is perfect, a Christian just knows that a lot of things are out of our control and we know who is in control; our Lord and Savior Jesus Christ. We know when we sin and then genuinely repent, forgiveness is given by God.

For anyone who thinks that means you can just keep sinning purposely and keep repenting and think everything is fine is missing the point. For one, God knows your heart. He knows if and when you are genuine; you can fool people but you cannot fool God because only he can judge you. He has never let man down so that alone allows you to be uncommon and live a different life for the better; like I said, not easier. If you're not ready for that responsibility, to give to God the glory, maybe Christianity is not for you and that's perfectly fine. When you do accept being a Christian and don't live accordingly or you critique other Christians and even other religions or non-believers, you are pushing people away from what you're trying to preach and it gives them good reasons to not be attracted to what you believe in.

Christians critique Christians or "church people" but claim they want others to become Christians, what sense does that make? That's like saying, "Hey I'm on this team but I don't like John. He's the team captain but he's a hypocrite and isn't what he seems. His brother, who everyone thinks is the best player, doesn't practice hard but you should come join our team." I can't speak for anyone else but if I heard something like that, I would get as far away from that person and their team as possible after declining to join their team; that is the problem with religion, it's simply the people. It becomes counter-productive in a sense; people don't want to be a part of something that's heavily criticized because it's hard. It's like people only rooting for a team when they're winning or jumping on the bandwagon; it's all fun and easy when you're winning and things are going well. Christianity is to the extreme and many religions, period, as far as being constantly criticized so the challenge isn't for everyone and that's the reality of it.

For whatever reason that still boggles my mind, people would just rather be negative instead of positive, even if it's about their own beliefs. It's a sad thing because we should all stand for something that's bigger than us, for its good and bad or we will fall for anything. I'm not sure if we fully understand how powerful negativity can be, whether we realize it or not. Now I'm not saying that Christianity doesn't have problems, especially the people who represent it because it does. But when a family has problems what happens? It's discussed and stays within the family, not with outsiders. In today's society whether it's issues with religions, relationships, jobs, or anything else when problems arise we don't discuss them with the people we have the issue with, we go to social networks or gossip to people who have nothing to do with the situation. This is what makes Christianity unattractive and not inspiring in the least bit.

I truly pray that you don't let one bad experience with religion, church, love, failure, divorce, or anything else discourage you and make you believe that good doesn't exist in all of these things; you can find light and purpose in anything if you look for it. There is no such thing as darkness, there's only a lack of light. Before you judge anyone or anything, if you don't have anything good to say, don't say it, otherwise, be a part of the solution and that should be all there is to it. Be that light to shine on all of the darkness that exists in this world.

Now, it should be the other way around; it should inspire the good and not push people to think Christianity is dysfunctional and unattractive when in fact it's the people in it. No different than everyone's family, we all have that family member or members that, let's say, we just wish they would do better because we know they can. No matter what they do, they still have the same last name and the same blood as you so when they do something fair or unfair, your entire family name is put through the dirt. Christianity is no different. The religion is criticized so much by non-believers that it causes "believers" to criticize and say things like, "I'm a Christian but I'm not like the church people" or "I believe in God but I don't have to go to church to get to heaven" or "These preachers are this or that and church just isn't for me, but I am a Christian."

I cannot say this enough, people make it out to be the religion as if it's flawed but if flaws do arise, it's the people. Still, this is no excuse for a Christian to act in such a way. No one ever said being a Christian would be easy but it is said to make your life better.

I understand there's "bad" preachers and churches out there that have no business representing God, I get all that, I'm not referring to them. But people from the outside looking in criticizing, their opinions are actually irrelevant if we put this in perspective. Put it like this, a person outside of your family (non-believer) tries to critique your household family (Christians) but they don't live with you or live like you. That makes their opinions irrelevant because they're literally ignorant to what you're going through and how you're trying to live. Some may know more than others but no one can actually experience and feel and relate to you and your family unless they're a part of it.

Now, let's say it's someone who used to practice Christianity and no longer does, well that's fine. If they had a "bad" experience and no longer believe in it but cannot continue their life without trying to talk negative about something they used to be a part of and live by, well that says a lot more about them than the religion itself because misery loves company. Why waste time and energy on something you don't agree with? Get a life. Non-believer's criticism only becomes relevant when us so called "believers" start to listen and agree and start our own criticizing about our family with someone outside of the family; that's killing your family.

I've always been a firm believer that you're either all in something or all out, there's no in between. To be a Christian or a part of anything that's much bigger than you are, it's almost certain that you won't agree with how everything is done but you keep that in house and discuss it within the family, not people outside of it. It just shows how much faith you have in your faith. For example, if you work and you dislike some things at your job but you need it to pay bills and take care of your children. You don't like how the boss does things or how they run the business but the cons of it don't outweigh the pros because at the end of the day, the job is helping you. Now, some may be thinking, "Well a job is different. You need money to live, you don't need religion" and that's your personal opinion and you're entitled to that. I only speak for myself when I say this: I need my religion, it has made me who I am and molding me at this very moment to be the better person I will become and strive for daily.

My faith in my religion will and has taken care of my needs financially, socially, spiritually, and everything else. I've never given away anything from my time or finances to my religion that hasn't been given back to me by God in a blessing that money could never buy. This is just my personal experience so it's what works for me and that is why I compared the job and religion. For the record, I don't care what someone in my family does or how bad it is, I can talk about them but if anyone else outside of my family tries to talk bad about them in front of me, then we're going to have a problem. Right or wrong, that's just me and I feel the same way about being a Christian; stand for something or fall for anything. Disagreeing and disrespect are two different things.

The way issues are discussed in society today with everyone else except the person whom the issue is with is just a common thing now. It honestly doesn't surprise me how religions get divided from one another and how Christians gossip about other Christians. That's not only killing religions but it's killing our families, schools, relationships, and the list goes on. I truly believe that there's nothing wrong with religions, it's the people in it; it's nothing wrong with relationships, it's the people in it; it's nothing wrong with love, it's the people in it; it's nothing wrong with this world, it's the people in it; it's nothing wrong with your life, it's the people you allow and keep in it! Do you see what I'm getting at here? When you keep negativity around then negativity will keep coming around in your life. Negativity tends to grow like weeds, you don't even have to do anything and weeds will grow so you have to constantly put effort in keeping it out once it comes; negativity is just like weeds.

I believe 100% that humans like to point the finger instead of simply just looking in the mirror and then when the finger gets pointed back at us, we get offended. When that happens, it's not even about the problem anymore, the issue becomes lost and another issue arises and nothing ever gets resolved. As much as I've discussed religion thus far in this book, it's not about religion; it's simply about achieving greatness, being wealthy, happy, healthy, and successful. Religion may fall under that for you but that doesn't mean that my ulterior motive is to make you religious. I am a Christian so everything I do, Christianity will be a part of that and that will always remain. I hope and pray you believe in a higher power; your relationship with the Most High is most important. More important than your pastor and your church because that's simply between you and him; everything else in between will be flawed because at the end of the day, we're human.

I simply want to inspire you to become a better you and give you the inspiration to go out and get whatever it takes to become that, whether it's religion or not. I just felt I owe it to my audience who supported me and believed in me by reading my book to discuss myself and my beliefs because I want to be honest and transparent with you. I want to let you know that my spirituality, religion, values, and beliefs are a big part of me and everything I do, including writing this book. Whether we are the same religion or not, agree or disagree about religion, this book is to inspire you for positive things even when the world presents negativity. If it's Christianity, great! If it's to chase a dream, then that's great also. I personally don't care what it is long as it's positive because positive energy is so contagious and if I help at least one person by writing this book, I know they will help someone else and the cycle will continue.

I do know that it's more than one thing that inspires people and I'm living proof of that, my religion isn't my only inspiration. It can be anything from movies, music, religion, poetry, art, people, experiences, and my personal favorite, books, but the list goes on. So whatever inspires you, find that then pass it on and that positive energy will never be lost. I don't want to be a hypocrite and tell you to do something that I'm not doing myself so I have to tell you what inspires me on a daily basis. What inspires me is simply inspiring others, there's nothing else that gives me more joy! It's a gift and my calling from God; I thank Him for it and take on the responsibility that comes with it and that is why I am writing this book, for YOU not for me.

I don't care how many book sales I get, as long as I can help make at least one person's life better by using my gift with words. I just pray that you find inspiration in this book to be who and what you want to be, not that I have all the answers to your questions because I, myself, have more questions than answers; I'm on a journey to get better just like you. I have never achieved anything in life, big or small, without starting with faith in God that He will create an opportunity that I'm preparing for beyond my control and believing in myself and my ability to take advantage of the opportunity.

# THE AVERAGE JOE

I've never been a fan of math class while going to school. I was never bad at math but I just was never too fond of it. Well I take that back. In college I was horrible in my statistics class, I had to take it twice and ended up with a "C". Honestly, that was the hardest grade I've ever worked for in my life. Between tutors daily and one of my fraternity brothers, who was an engineer major, putting the pressure on me to succeed, I definitely wouldn't have passed that class. Besides stats, I always thought math was simple; I never thought you had to be too smart to figure out math problems. Some people have gifts with numbers and some people are slower than others. I thought everyone could understand math problems at their own pace, it really never made me think so I was never a fan of it. As I grew older math would become one of my biggest life lessons.

When you take care of all of the small problems with the numbers, they will always solve the bigger problem; that's a fact that will always remain. In algebra when there's a long problem with many steps, you have to take that problem, break it down, and do each step one by one with its correct solution for each part and it'll all come together at the end. Is this starting to sound familiar to anyone? THIS IS WHAT LIFE IS ALL ABOUT! In life if you want to do great things, you must first do small things with great efficiency and effort. You can't just get the big number without properly handling the small numbers; in other words, we have to crawl before we walk. I have no idea why it's a part of human nature for us to tend to look over the small things and think the bigger things are more important.

We tend to hold back our greatest efforts until the "big opportunities" come around but that's not how you get the most out of life. *He that is faithful in that which is least is faithful also in much: and he that is unjust in the least is unjust also in much. Luke 16:10* It's like, if you give your child $20 and they spend it irresponsibly, why would you trust them with a $1,000? The answer is you wouldn't. It just doesn't make any sense and how you wouldn't trust your child, we are children of God, so why would he trust us with bigger blessings if he cannot trust us with smaller ones.

I do not believe in luck but I do agree with one definition I once read of luck: luck is when preparation meets opportunity. I love this because if that's what luck is, then I believe in that. Luck is not random, even though that's how most people make it out to be; that's not the luck I believe in but I believe in the definition I just stated. All the little things in your life and tests you go through are things preparing you for a bigger opportunity that will arise and it will expose how faithful you were in the small things. Now, this isn't about winning and losing because that's a state of mind; everyone that "wins" doesn't mean they've succeeded and everyone that "loses" doesn't mean they've "failed."

What I'm talking about is did you prepare and take small things seriously in practice and in life to prepare for game day when the big opportunity presents itself? Practice is those small elementary addition math problems that everyone knew and basically blurted out the answers before the teacher could finish the questions; they annoy you and you just want to move on to the more challenging things. That's life, but we tend to forget that these little things and steps are necessary. If we do not learn nor master the small addition, we can never move on to algebra, calculus, or even the dumb statistic math. We must focus on these small things because they will eventually add up to be a bigger blessing and a greater opportunity.

Let's look at the greats such as Michael Jordan and Jerry Rice. They said these two individuals were always the first to practice and the last to leave. Now, there's not too many people that have walked this planet (arguably) who could play basketball better than Michael Jordan or play wide receiver and catch a football better than Jerry Rice. Yet, these two guys were the most dedicated to something as small as practice. Michael and Jerry knew that if they didn't treat the practice like it was a championship game then they weren't giving themselves the best opportunity to take advantage of "luck" (when preparation meets opportunity) when it arrived. Does that mean Jordan made every game winning shot? No. Does that mean Jerry Rice caught every touchdown pass? No, not at all. But it's not hard to tell when the pressure gets going who's built for the situation and who isn't.

Greatness, success, and living life as a champion is not a switch you turn on only on game days but instead it's in everything you do; it's an everyday lifestyle, not some accomplishment. Your results cannot be perfect but your efforts can. If we fall in love with success and not the process of success, we will never become great at anything because we're only chasing the results, the big numbers, praise, and those bigger math problems. What we fail to realize as humans is that the process of success is so long that it takes up the majority of our time, yet we just want to chase the "success" that only lasts very briefly until we're moving on and chasing something else. I'm not saying don't strive for success but I am saying don't get caught up in it.

If you're in the season in your life to still be focused on little math addition problems then focus on that and master that, not until you get it right but until you can't get it wrong. Success is nothing more than what you do and how you feel about what you're doing. Don't let your success dictate how the world views you or you'll spend your entire life seeking the world's praise; in other words, "living for the people". Let others label you "successful" because that's their job, just smile and say thank you and keep your focus on getting better every day.

I always look at Michael Jordan and wonder did he ever really believe his own success and how good he was? I feel like if he did, there's no way he could've remained as hungry as he was year after year to become a champion again. I came to the conclusion that MJ was addicted to the process of success; the challenge and not success itself. He loved the journey and everything about it. Just think of the years and years that Michael Jordan practiced and trained for basketball, yet in reality he only won 6 championships. Now, that's a lot more than a lot of people (I know it's not the most by one individual but Mike is arguably the greatest), my point is that his dedication more so made him the greatest than his 6 championships. MJ wanted championships more than anyone but I believe his drive for that is what made him "MJ" because if that wasn't the case, then why is he the greatest and not Bill Russell who has more rings? (This is my opinion.) This is exactly my point. The fact that he doesn't have the most rings and is in the argument of being the greatest should tell us something.

You don't necessarily have to like the process to success but you better know it's necessary to get where you want to be and you ought to know you'll spend more time in it than in your "success". This is success in itself and that's where people get confused. If you only focus on the results of what you're doing that simply means you don't love what you're doing enough. If you don't love what you're doing, you won't give it your all because you're only looking to get something out of it instead of putting everything into it. If and when you put everything into succeeding, only then will you get everything out of it. You have to give before you receive. It goes back to that basic elementary math; once you learn to give great effort, master, and have fun with those little numbers, you can eventually play with bigger numbers and handle them properly.

You don't want to get to the big numbers of success and become overwhelmed; you only become overwhelmed when you're not properly prepared. The one thing I hear from a lot of successful people, and it shows if you pay attention, is that the only thing worse than not being successful is being successful once (a one hit wonder), tasting it, and not being able to repeat that success again. If you pay attention to the small things and focus on the process, there should be no reason that you cannot duplicate your success. Most of us think we know the small math so well and think we're ready for the bigger math that we get there and "feel" successful, but arriving does not mean you're successful because when you get there the work has just begun.

A lot of people get that opportunity but it's harder to stay at the top versus just getting there. That's why the process is so important and that's why you have to be a little "crazy" to fall in love with this process; it's uncomfortable and like I said, we as humans like to be comfortable. We think that if we work hard, we eventually arrive and get to relax; I mean you can do that but looking back on what you've done will leave you left behind, looking back while running will only slow you down. I'm not saying not to be proud of what you've accomplished but you have to look at every day as a challenge to get better at something. There really aren't any off days in life if you want to be better than the average Joe and become the greatest.

Let's think about a large and long algebra problem that we have to break down and do step by step, there's always some basic elementary addition and subtraction in these problems. We can work through this entire problem that can take 10 minutes but if we forget to add or subtract something the correct way, then all of the other work we do is irrelevant. We did all of the big problems correct but we didn't master the small things, this is why small things are so important and why we should give them great efforts every single day. Now, this is coming from myself, a very competitive individual and it's just in my nature and it's just who I am. To the contrary, we all want comfort in something and life cannot be all about work and chasing something, there has to be some kind of comfort and contentment, otherwise, you'll spend your entire life chasing instead of living. But the problem arises when we seek that comfort in "success" or how people view us on what we've accomplished; it shouldn't take for someone else to praise you for you to be proud and happy about who you are. Key words "who you are" not "what you've done." There are people who truly love you for who you are not what you've done; there's a big difference.

I've driven myself crazy with my work ethic, working so hard to get better every day to achieve goals and dreams or what not. It took for God to put me in a situation where all I had was him to find comfort for me to realize that he is the only one I can find comfort in. It doesn't matter where I work, what I accomplish, or what people think of me, I will be able to have my mind, body, and spirit at peace with who I am. The Lord created me to be who I am so it is my maker who most understands me because he created me. Psalm 62:1-2 says, *My soul finds rest in God alone; my salvation comes from him. He alone is my rock and my salvation; he is my fortress, I will never be shaken.* Now, this doesn't change my efforts in everything I do, small or big, but it did change my attitude towards my results and what I thought "success" actually was.

One of my favorite scriptures says, *I know both how to be abased, and I know how to abound: everywhere and in all things I am instructed both to be full and to be hungry, both to abound and to suffer need. Philippians 4:12* This scripture is so simple yet so complex that it took me quite some time to grasp what it really means. How can one be both hungry and full? To me, it means that Michael Jordan never stopped trying to get better. He wanted greatness and championships more than anything but when you give your all and things don't work out as planned, then you can be content with that because everything happens for a reason; God has a plan that was bigger than ours in the first place.

If Michael Jordan would've let the Pistons beating him in the conference finals all those years discourage him, then MJ may not be who he is today. Instead, he kept up the great effort and eventually got over that hump. This doesn't mean that we will not get what we're pursuing but it doesn't mean it'll happen on our time or how we envisioned it happening; God will often give us something even better. To be hungry and full means to always get better daily and go after what we want but be thankful for what The Most High has already blessed us with; this scripture is based all on perspective.

# SUCCESS

### *Success is Overrated*

*I finally figured out that success is a direction and not
a destination
The irony in knowing that I can never reach it is the fuel
of my motivation.
I'm chasing a perfection that can't be perfected, I'm chas-
ing success but I don't know the definition.
People say success is what you make it, but the illusion of
thinking you are can cause you to be complacent.
If you reach and touch success where do you go after that?
When you reach the top of the mountain it's only downhill
after that.
The mountain never stops going up, failing doesn't mean
I've lost, winning doesn't mean I've won, chasing things
that run from you but success was never there to begin with.
The reality is that success is the effort you use to pursue
success to begin with.
Giving 100% is all I can live with, after that the results
are for God to sort out and deal with.
What it takes to become successful is far more important*

27

*than being successful;*
*Enjoy the process for it will teach you valuable life lessons*
*and you will live in abundance with blessings.*

*-Peris DeVohn*

The following is a poem I wrote once it finally hit me what this vague term "success" is all about. Success means different things to a lot of different people but I will go out on a limb and say most of us label success as being financially well off, accomplishing a dream or goal, and having this feeling that we have "arrived" where we've been yearning to be. I'm aware that some don't think this way. Some think success is becoming mature in their religion or walk with God, getting a career, creating that dream job, having a family, moving up out of poverty, and who knows what else because the list can be infinite. One of the questions I always had is what comes after we arrive or reach this destination we like to call "success" that we spend a big part of our lives chasing?

Just pay attention and observe the media and entertainment world. Look at all the pro athletes for example; you have tons of great collegiate athletes but when they get to the professional level, they become mediocre and sometimes don't even last in the pros, let alone become great. I always ask myself what is the difference between individuals like a Michael Jordan and an "average joe" when they get to the professional level? Now, let's say Average Joe had a rough childhood growing up in poverty and becoming a millionaire is the success that he wanted and that was his goal in professional sports. I'm here to tell you that there is absolutely nothing wrong with that if that's what you want out of life. But what is next? You can't play basketball forever and you cannot live off the high of only making it to the NBA; you have to set new goals and become great in the NBA and that takes more and probably harder work than it took to get there.

After you arrive at that and you've touched that success immediately, you become complacent and you don't have the same motivation to keep what you have that you had when you were chasing it (it's all about the journey), so it's inevitable everything and everyone will pass you by and you'll be looking around like what just happened. To continue using MJ as an example, I truly believe that Michael Jordan didn't want to become the greatest basketball player to ever live, I believe he wanted to become the best player Michael Jordan could possibly be and being the greatest of all time came along with it. I will explain the difference.

At some point Michael Jordan had become the greatest player to ever play basketball while still playing, no different than Average Joe arriving to the NBA and reaching his dream. Now, when Jordan arrived at this point, if his only goal was to become the greatest instead of also wanting to become the greatest Jordan he could possibly be, then Jordan's game would've declined because his motivation would've been gone. In Jordan's case, he didn't sell himself short, he had more goals and more motivation because his expectations for himself were greater than just becoming the greatest of all time. Although, others labeled him that and that's what he constantly heard he didn't fall into what I like to call the "success trap".

Let's stop and think about this a little deeper. If the entire world is calling you the greatest then dammit you're the greatest, but the question I have is how do you ignore that and not be complacent and want to be greater? I think if we're told how good we are long enough, we'll eventually start to smell ourselves and believe it. If you're the greatest and you want to be greater than the greatest that means you want to be better than yourself; it takes a unique individual to think this way but that is what Jordan was, the ultimate competitor.

I'm not saying that Jordan didn't believe he was the greatest, what I'm saying is that Jordan kept things in perspective and somehow kept the motivation to stay hungry, to keep improving his game, and to keep winning. All that means is that the only competition is yourself! No one else matters, not even their opinions telling you that you're the greatest because if you feel you're the greatest, then you believe that and others who are like you were when you were trying to become the greatest will catch you; but not Michael Jordan. I think it's harder to stay the best than to become the best. Michael Jordan is so special because he knew that it was all about the journey. He kept setting more goals for himself and that's what he thrived off of.

I read in a book where Michael Jordan said, "I had to give my best every night because I always thought someone may be watching me play for the first time." Now, this is Michael Jordan I'm talking about. I'm sure just about everyone in the world had seen him play at that point in his career but MJ knew how to self-motivate, which is so important. That is an example of how you make your own motivation to keep giving it your all. Michael Jordan retired from basketball as the greatest ever and decided to go play pro baseball, a sport he hadn't played in years and he was not good at anymore, why? I'll tell you why! It's the journey, the new challenge and effort it took for him to become better and reach a new goal; he liked the challenge. He had reached a point in basketball, I think, to where he didn't feel that same challenge to constantly get better. (They said MJ was the first to show up to baseball practice and the last one to leave every single day.) Another thing that going to play baseball says about Jordan is that he's not afraid of starting over with a new task from a humble beginning.

Most people in today's world fear starting all over more than death even. People get stuck and comfortable in jobs that they actually hate or relationships that are not healthy and years of their lives are wasted because of the fear of starting over and facing the unknown. This isn't about whether you're successful at something or not but more about whether your heart is still in what you're doing. I think MJ's heart wasn't in basketball anymore, despite at the prime of his career he needed a new challenge; that's true character and doing what's best for you being a "me-pleaser".

Can you imagine voluntarily going from arguably the greatest ever at one sport to another sport where you (for lack of better terms) suck? It makes no sense to the outside world because only an ultimate competitor would understand such a thing. Once you feel you've arrived and you start to smell yourself and feel successful then you no longer like challenges. You feel you've already overcome the challenge and became "successful" like Average Joe making it to the pros and becoming wealthy. These are two totally different mindsets.

Jordan likes to constantly challenge himself (which in my opinion is success), even when he has already reached the greatest because he knows the challenge and competition is within himself, not other athletes. Even if others label him the greatest, that's irrelevant because he didn't want to become the greatest NBA player, he wanted to become the greatest Michael Jordan he could be at everything he did; not just basketball. Jordan knew that success is not a destination but a journey of constant and conscious effort. It's not only a mindset and competitive spirt but it's the choice not to get caught up in "success". It's realizing that the journey is everything and knowing that is success in itself. Success is something you live on a daily basis, not something you become.

The journey to every goal is where you will spend most of your time anyway so you might as well embrace it and enjoy it. If you cannot enjoy and embrace the journey but you think the destination will fulfill your desire, then when you arrive you may be happy and temporarily on a high; that feeling will fade as fast as buying a new car because you put all your feeling of self-worth in something that's outside of you and bet it on your happiness and fulfillment. That is why a lot of entertainers, professional athletes, and "successful people" arrive to their dreams and have more success and money than they could ever spend but are the most depressed and unhappy people on the planet; some of them even commit suicide.

A lot of people are motivated and driven to succeed to make themselves feel good about themselves, which can be the ultimate motivator these days but in my opinion, it's the wrong one. In today's world, everyone is motivated by their haters. Now, I'm not saying that's good or bad but if you're not wanting to do something for yourself, then you're going to live your life trying to impress people. You can only impress people when someone is paying you attention, so where does your motivation come from after you've proved these people wrong? There is none. You hit a wall because you weren't doing it for yourself first and that's the beginning of success finding, out what you want to do for you and why.

Think about that; they arrived at their goal and got everything they ever wanted and asked for but yet cannot even be happy with it. I am not saying that you don't celebrate and enjoy all of your accomplishments, big or small, because life is hard and all of your successes deserve a pat on the back or some form of acknowledgment but most of all you should be proud of yourself. All I'm saying is that enjoy the people, experiences, good and bad times, situations, and everything else on that journey to get there. When you get there and feel you've become successful, immediately set new goals to keep that same hunger it took to get there. There are no arriving moments at anything in life. No matter how good we think we are, we cannot stop practicing and challenging ourselves to become better.

We all know the saying that you either get better or worse every day, well I halfway agree with that statement. The reality is that we really don't get worse, other people just get better and pass us by because of our complacency; we stay the same and others get better. People like Michael Jordan constantly challenge themselves no matter the accomplishments they reach because they know it's never over and getting better and enjoying the journey is the only way a fulfilled life can be lived.

*"Success is not final, failure is not fatal: it's the courage to continue that counts"*

-*Winston S. Churchill*

I always compare the journey to success to a road trip somewhere with family or friends. I'm sure we all can relate that the journey to the destination seems to take up more time than the vacation within itself, even if it's not the case. I always wondered why does it feel that way? Before you know it, you're back in the car on the highway heading home discussing who will drive first because everyone is tired. I also observed that when taking these road trips that all conversations, no matter what they are about, become very interesting and it's all laughs, disagreements, agreements, opinions, and everything you can think of but the best way to describe it is just fun.

Why do we appreciate the conversation and company of friends and family more while on a road trip? Why do we all talk about the journey and the people who've been on it with us when we arrive and become a pro athlete or a bestselling author or win a championship? I think it's obvious; the journey is the most important part of life and every part of it. Everyone loves to talk about memories and the good times or the journey, as I like to call it. What I think we as humans fail to realize and the reason we can't stop talking about the past and good memories (not that it's a bad thing) is because we didn't enjoy them like we should've when they were present. We fail to realize that the memories we talk about, if we would've learned to enjoy them when they were present, are ones that we could be enjoying for the second time through reminiscing. We could've enjoyed them while we were making them and we could've enjoyed them when we grow older while reminiscing. I think most of us, including myself, fail to do this simple but powerful thing, to just live and be conscious in the present, to enjoy the right now. The right now is the most important time there is, which will be discussed in more depth later.

I'll use a funeral for an example to elaborate on the point I'm trying to get across. I know you may link funerals to a time of mourning and sadness, which it may be, but it's really supposed to be a time of reflection and a celebration of a person's life (journey) and the birth of them going to live in eternity. The mourning and sadness comes from our own selfish reasons from missing that person, which we all have the right to do. I use a funeral because it's the best and most extreme example to use to prove that it's all about the journey. Just think, at a funeral when someone gets up to talk about the individual, what do they talk about? They don't talk about or focus on how they died or the day of their birth. They talk about everything they did in life, the journey, whether it's what they contributed to the world or the impact they had on that person talking specifically. It's a reflection of their life and what is life?

Life is the JOURNEY between birth and death. Think about it, one day we all are born and one day we will all die; that's a fact, end of story, not my opinion. All that matters in life when we think about it is what we do in between those two occurrences; that's life and that is what really counts. It doesn't matter what situation you were born into, it doesn't matter how you left this world, whether it was of old age, sickness, or other causes, it only matters what we do in between to have a positive impact on someone else's life and to leave the world a better place.

Just think about when someone dies; how they die may affect the grieving process to an extent to the surviving family as in an old grandmother dying who was expected to versus a younger person dying for whatever reason beyond our understanding. At the end of the day, it really doesn't matter because dead is dead. The person who is dead doesn't know the difference, God has them in a better place and they no longer feel any physical pain.

Now, as I was writing this talking about death, which I'm trying to be as honest as possible without coming off too harsh but I will always be honest, the question popped in my head about kids and babies dying. Why do babies, kids, and any young person that we "feel" is too young to die, die? Why does God allow that to happen? I think most of us question God in a sense as to why these things take place. Well, I don't know the answer because I believe it's something that God has beyond any human understanding most of the time. I do think it's for a reason, for the better; this is not me being an optimist which I am, but this is me having faith in something that's bigger than me, which is my Lord and Savior Jesus Christ. If we understood and could make sense of everything then there would be no purpose for there to be a God to serve. At the end of the day why would we need God if we understood everything?

When people die young or when we "feel" it was too early for them to leave this world, just think how it changes our perspective on life. For most people, it brings families, friends, and loved ones closer. It makes you want to tell people you love that you love them more often, it makes you alert and aware that some things are beyond our control. But my question is why do we as humans feel like we are in control? We tend to think people will be here forever, even though we know that it is a fact that everyone will die. We get used to things and don't cherish the moment and enjoy the journey with that person because we think tomorrow always exist, which is false.

Tomorrow never exist; it's always today, which I'll later elaborate on in another chapter. We tend to naturally think without even trying to that a person won't die until they get old. We as humans are scared to accept the fact that someone can die right now or tomorrow or the next day; the fact that when you see a family member or friend that can be the last time you ever see them. That's not negative thinking, that's reality. That doesn't mean live scared, it simply means live every day like it's your last and ENJOY THE JOURNEY with everyone in your life. We're all born on a specific date that we all know but our death date is one that remains unknown. We don't know when that time will come, so we have to enjoy time as it comes; that means on a day to day basis. That means we shouldn't hold grudges or let little disagreements with friends or family cause us to lose time with one another because you can never get it back.

When we lose someone, we always say, "Man, I wish I could've just said this or did that, or just let them know I loved, adored, looked up to them." It's a sad thing with us humans, we really don't know what we have until it's gone and as cliché as it sounds, it's true. That journey you have in your life with everyone who is

36

included in it will be the best success and fulfillment you will ever have, because that means you are consciously living in and enjoying the present and that is real joy. I'm not saying this will cause you to be happy at a funeral when you lose a loved one, but most people mourn not for the person dying but because they didn't take advantage of the time when that person was living. We mourn for our own selfish reasons than of those of the one who died. That person could have been in a physical state of pain and we still don't want to let them go but why? Because it's so much we didn't say or time we should've spent with them or time we did spend and didn't enjoy it. It's called regret. We regret that we didn't enjoy the journey with that individual and that is a hard pill to swallow for anyone, I don't care who you are; I know from first-hand experience.

Back to the question about the kids, I think when death occurs with kids, or even babies, before they ever had a chance to have a life, it is simply to teach us to cherish life even more. Death has no prejudice. I think that kid's lives are sacrificed to teach us adults that we aren't living right, we aren't loving the people in our lives, we aren't taking advantage of time, we aren't enjoying the journey and the blessing called life that we have right before our own eyes. When a child dies, that perspective instantly changes! But why? Enjoying the journey isn't an easy task, it takes constant and conscious effort. At other times, unfortunately, it may take a death of a loved one or someone we "think" shouldn't die to shift our perspective about enjoying our journey and what and who we already have. I believe, God uses us and our situations for a bigger picture that he's painting for us, or should I say a bigger blessing.

Nothing or anyone will ever replace anyone old or young when they die, but it may teach you to love your other loved ones better. It may teach you to enjoy life more and everything you already have and not to focus on too much that you don't have; to simply enjoy the ride. I'm a firm believer that happiness cannot be in tomorrow if tomorrow isn't promised and it's a fact that every day tomorrow isn't promised so, therefore, enjoy the journey and be happy RIGHT NOW in today. Tomorrow's goals won't bring you anything worthy that you can't already possess. We have to focus on not letting it take such extremes to shift our thinking and enjoy our journey while we are in it.

*"Success isn't owned, it's leased and the rent is due every single day."*

*- JJ Watt*

# THE JOURNEY

*"People tend to think success is some destination, I couldn't disagree more. Success is a lifestyle and more of a direction. If you value who you are and value what you do, then you'll change lives for the better every single day; that's success. God gave you a gift to master so you can bless others; that's your success."*

*- Peris DeVohn*

The journey itself can be so many different things. The quality of your journey will be a reflection of the quality of your attitude about your own personal journey. The best part about that is that our attitude is a choice. It's a choice we make every single day and most of us don't even realize it. We tend to let our day or whatever happens in it set the tone for our attitude, instead of letting our attitude set the tone for our day. We fail to realize that how we respond to things is more important than anything that actually happens to us. From the moment we wake up, we can make an aggressive and very intentional decision that it will be a great day. Why must we wait on something to trigger our own happiness and greatness within? Who made up that rule and why do so many of us follow this rule?

In this thing called life, you have to claim things because hope alone is not enough. When you only hope for things, that means you're timid and you don't want what you "claim" you want bad enough yet. I'm not saying there isn't a time for hope itself because it is; sometimes that may be all you have left when life has beat you up. The long-term goal should be the faith to claim what you want before you actually have it. It doesn't matter who you are, when you set out to fly and live your dreams it's going to be hard and life is going to knock you down. When you claim it's going to be done and you make that decision, you will be willing to keep pushing through the tough times and adversity. No one has ever achieved great things that didn't have to overcome great obstacles. I've studied a lot of successful people and that's just how it works. Why? I don't know, but that's just how it is.

I also know from my short time on this earth thus far and the little success I've experienced, that you have to pay and work hard for everything. This is not a secret nor is it rocket science. Successful people are willing to sacrifice their todays to build greatness for tomorrow; they understand and completely accept what delayed gratification is all about. They know success isn't always convenient, comfortable, or easy, nor does it happen overnight. I've also observed that when successful people decide what they want to do, they don't even know exactly how they're going to do it. Having everything figured out about the journey to your destination just isn't realistic and even if you do plan it, it's not going to play out how you thought. You can still get there and YOU WILL if you don't quit. It's something you just learn from trial and error along the way, but the process makes you stronger and better by adapting to the obstacles you didn't plan for.

I also believe that God knows us better than we know ourselves and I believe he knows that if we knew up front what it will take to get to where we're going, that most of us wouldn't have the guts to even start; we'll quit before we even try. Most of us don't know what it will take to get there and we still quit or even fail to begin, so I'm not sure whether we would fear known difficulty or the mystery of failing or succeeding; I honestly haven't quite figured that one out yet. The thing we must always remember is that knowing what you want is more important than knowing how you're going to get it, that will always play itself out if you just take a leap of faith and take a step in the direction you want to go.

Our journey is very vital to our growth, maturity, and our success to be able to handle and sustain it. This is our greatest strength because our journey is a one of one, designed for us to be mastered by us. If we don't go through this journey the right way, then we will not become all of whom we need to be to add value to others lives by sharing our blessings. One cannot achieve unreasonable happiness if one doesn't go through this journey with the right attitude. A lot of things during this journey may not even make sense at the time but in due time they will. God knows how many failures we can handle and how many we need to be ready to handle our blessings and successes. Of course, we as humans don't see it that way. We want what we want right this second but the reality is that life doesn't work that way, as we should all know by now. So what should we do in the in between time when the journey is tough and it's not making any sense?

This is the perfect time to build our relationship with the Lord and have faith that what we're going through will not be wasted. This is also the perfect time to appreciate the people who are supporting you and giving you motivation throughout this journey because those people are blessings themselves in your life. Please, we must remember to give them the appreciation they deserve sooner than later. No matter how bad life gets, God is always up to something for the better; his blueprint for your life is flawless. We must not panic when trouble or a storm arises during our journey but we must learn to be aware of what we need to learn and take with us from these experiences; they're meant for something even if we don't understand it at the time. Don't let life's situations distract you from where God wants to send you. He wants to send you somewhere that you're not quite ready for right this moment and he loves us so much that he will not put us in a situation, good or bad, that we're not ready to handle. Please, reread that last sentence, especially, the good or bad part.

If you're going through something, even if it "feels bad", you're strong enough to handle it and eventually, it'll work out for your good if you keep going. God loves us so much is the reason he does this; he knows a blessing at the wrong time can cause a long-term failure and mess up that blessing. He also knows that allowing us to go through hard times can properly prepare us for the blessing so we can appreciate it more and handle it better to keep it longer. It's no different than when you become an adult and start working for the things that you purchase for yourself and you tend to treat things better because you worked for it. While as a kid when your parents bought you everything, you treated things with less care because you didn't go through anything to get it, it was just handed to you. It's the same concept. We're God's children and he knows what's best, we just have to trust him during the process even when we don't quite understand it.

These things and the way of living are much easier to read and write rather than to actually apply to our lives; I currently struggle with everything I'm writing about. I hope that doesn't make me sound like a hypocrite but I'm still learning just like the next person. Just because something is difficult to achieve or master doesn't make it impossible, keep working at it to get better at it; it's that simple. If you really want to be unreasonably happy these are the necessary steps that we must take. If you only want to be happy when you accomplish goals or when everything is going well, then this may not be for you. Me, personally, I want to be happy as I can be all the time. I mean why can't I? Why aim for a 3.5 GPA when the highest you can get is a 4.0 on the scale? It just doesn't make sense to me to ever settle for less when it comes to anything in life. Always shoot for the stars and beyond and if you miss, you will fall nothing short of greatness each time if you give it all that you have. Even if you miss that 4.0, don't tie your self-worth to you not reaching that goal.

Setting goals are meant to keep you on track and motivated but most people set goals and do everything they can to accomplish them to feel worthy; that's a problem. When you accomplish goals, people will love you, clap for you, and give you a lot of attention but when that stops, which it will, then what will you do? Will you still be happy? If not, you'll just continue to chase that high and that is not good. In my opinion, it's just like a drug, if not worse; it's called fame. This is why I believe success doesn't equal happiness but happiness equals success. People who are unreasonably happy are happy and have an attitude of gratitude no matter where they are in life. Everything isn't perfect or the best but they find a way to make the best of everything in life no matter the situation.

I think the biggest misunderstanding of happy people is that others think they're content and are satisfied with where they are but that's not true. What people fail to realize is there's a difference between making the best of where you are and being satisfied with where you are. Why even complain about where you are? You are where you are and you can't take that back, you can only move forward. We are where we are today based on who we once were in the past and the decisions we made; we must accept that. People can't let go of their past that led them to where they are today and this cripples us from a brighter tomorrow. We will forgive someone we're in love with who constantly treats us like crap but won't forgive ourselves. If you want to grow, you have to let your old self go. If you want to be great, you have to let go of good; it's the only way.

Unreasonably happy people know how to use where they are as an advantage instead of using it as an excuse to remain stagnant. It's possible to be happy with what you currently have and still simultaneously be working towards more. In fact, I think it's healthy for your peace of mind to be happy with wherever you are in life and with however much you have. Whether it's a lot or a little, the glass is always half full. There's nothing wrong with wanting more, I'm not against that but what value are you placing on getting more? One thing I always try to keep in perspective is that someone in this world is happy with less than what I have and someone is unhappy with more than what I have. This attitude of gratitude will keep life in perspective for you the more you practice it.

If you're not where you want to be and if you take note of everything you did to get up to that point, then you have an advantage and you know what doesn't work. Knowledge and wisdom are two different things; knowledge is good but at the end of the day, knowledge alone isn't enough to get the job done. Wisdom is knowing how to apply that knowledge to your own personal life to make it better. Your journey to success is filled with wisdom through your various experiences. Understanding how we ended up where we are today is so important to getting to where we're trying to go tomorrow; a better place.

To deal with our past is not always an easy thing to do but it's what we need to do to set ourselves free to live the life we want to live. Guilt, regret, jealousy, envy, and not forgiving others cripples our own success and reaching our full-potential. We must let these things go if we want to move on and grow into someone better. Once we realize the power in freeing our minds, we can then start to plant seeds of success, greatness, and unreasonable happiness. Knowing what doesn't work is just as important as knowing what does.

"If I knew then what I know now." We all hear people say this all the time and for me, personally, it's annoying. Society today tends to frown upon people making mistakes but I don't. If you're making mistakes that means you're trying and learning. I would rather be an aggressive screw up in life (of course, with good intentions) and my experiences to learn from versus being a passive person who has never done anything because they always played it safe. If we did know then what we know now, would we be the unique individuals we are today? Why not take pride in our mistakes, growing pains, and temporary defeats? They say wise people learn from other's mistakes and this may be true, but I believe there's no better teacher than your own personal experiences.

Sometimes touching the fire and seeing how hot it is for yourself goes a much longer way than taking someone else's word about how hot it is. I think this is why parenting is so hard because parents naturally want to protect their children from everything that may harm them. You can be a perfect parent but the reality is that your kid will mess up and make mistakes. What's most important is that you encourage them to keep going more than you criticize them to the point to where they are afraid to make mistakes. We must learn to accept that kids are going to do the opposite of what you tell them to do because kids are naturally inquisitive. Not in all cases but in some cases more than we would like to accept, this is often times the best way to learn.

We also know this is no different for us adults. At one time or another in life, we've all had that friend and we've all been that friend as well that stays in a toxic relationship. Deep down we know this person isn't good for us. Everyone tells us plus, we're just not happy; it's obvious. This can be very frustrating to the friend who cares sincerely about us who we complain to and ask advice from constantly. This friend tells us the same thing over and over, to leave the relationship and we never do. Eventually, the friend will stop giving you advice because you're not taking it. That friend gets to the point and understands you're not going to leave the relationship until you're fed up, so they would rather just listen to you than to agree with something they don't agree with or keep giving advice that's ignored.

We've all been there until we're tired of getting burned in that toxic relationship for ourselves but we won't leave. Once we work up that courage to leave and accept the truth for what it is and stop fearing the unknown of change, we leave and never look back because of what that experience has taught us up to that point. When we get past these things, we often look back and reflect on how silly we once were and even laugh about it. Most of us only have to go through this one time to never put ourselves in a position to deal with this again. This doesn't mean you give up on relationships, it just means you have different standards and bottom lines now that you're not willing to compromise on based off your experience. Someone telling you something isn't always enough, even if they're 100% right; experience is the best teacher there is and ever will be.

This is why people who experience failure the most are the most successful people; they know what it's like to be at the bottom. They've made so many mistakes and ended up where they didn't want to be so often that it was only a matter of time until they succeeded as long as they didn't become discouraged from their temporary failures. Experience taught them more than knowledge could ever teach them. You ever know someone who's extremely book smart but couldn't survive in a real life crisis or adversity? We all know people like this and it's not bad, nor is it their fault, it's just the way the cookie crumbles from lack of experience. Reading and having information from books isn't enough if you cannot apply it to your reality. Just because you read books about someone else's experience and their success, it's not going to make you successful just because you know their story and what they did.

I've read hundreds of self-help, biographies and auto-biographies about success. To be quite honest with you, they all pretty much say the same thing; you fail and if you love what you're doing enough, you keep going and don't quit until you succeed. No matter what you do in life you're going to have obstacles but your passion has to be greater than your adversity. Most of us have the knowledge to know what it takes to be successful and live the life we want to live but we just lack the discipline and consistency with the actions it takes to get it done. That or we haven't had such an experience with failure to the point we're sick and tired of being sick and tired and we understand if there's a will there's a way if we want it bad enough. We haven't experienced failure enough to the point we stop fearing it and the great Tony Robbins call this a breakthrough.

Like I said, I've read so many motivational books to the point I lost count and they all run together. I had so much knowledge stored in my brain I couldn't believe it. It wasn't until I experienced my own temporary defeat in life to where I began to actively start using that knowledge in my own life as wisdom and I was able to apply it. Me reading about someone else's experience wasn't enough; me knowing their story inside and out doesn't make it my own. I had to have my own experiences to be able to go to that next level; reading a book alone couldn't give me that. So we must learn to break this habit as humans of being ashamed of temporary defeats and mistakes. The hardest part about evolving and continuing to grow as a person is being comfortable with being uncomfortable.

Weight lifting, thanks to gravity, doesn't always feel good but when your body starts to show the results from your work, you train your mind to like the pain in a weird way because you know the results it'll bring. While you're on those last few repetitions, lifting the weights and the lactic acid feels like fire in your muscles and your body is done physically but mentally, you push pass your comfort zone because you know this is the exact moment where the growth takes place. Life is literally no different, the weight just comes in different forms, failures, setbacks, mistakes, doubts, stress, and anything else that can cause resistance during your journey. Just think when you're lifting weights, what do you naturally want to do so you'll feel better and the burning will go away? You want to stop because when you put the weights down, your muscles begin to recover and stop burning.

It's okay to take a break and gather yourself when life gets tough but make sure you always come back for more; expecting the pain that it takes for growth to take place. The recipe for success and a great body is not going to change; work gets you the results you want and if you're not constantly challenging yourself, you will never grow and that's a fact. This is not something I made up personally or that I've discovered, this is the reality of it that was here before me and will continue to be long after me.

I'm not writing this to make you "feel" better or get you "pumped" up about how to change your situation, I wrote this to help you take control and change your situation. Acting off of feelings alone never last long enough to get you the results that you want. We must learn to face and accept the truth. We will not always feel like doing what we know it will take to get to where we want but we have to train our body and our minds to proceed to do what needs to be done. Making a plan and actually executing that plan are two totally different things; there are levels to success and any level skipped and not executed correctly will have to be done over again in order to achieve unreasonable happiness and success.

# TODAY AND RIGHT NOW

*"If we wait until we're ready, we'll be waiting the rest of our lives. There's only two days in the year that nothing can be done. One is called yesterday. The other is called tomorrow."*

*- Dalai Lama*

Time may be the only thing in life that's never wrong. The time is always right to do whatever you want but is the time ever right to do the wrong things? Does the absence of good mean the presence of bad? The point is that at the end of the day, time and how we use it is very important; regardless, to what you think of time and the pressure from it, the whole concept of time is irrelevant and let me explain why. If we knew when exactly our time was going to run out on this earth, then this chapter in this book would serve no purpose at all but that's not the case.

If we actually took time for what it really is, then there would be no procrastination. We procrastinate simply because one, we are lazy; we are the best at justifying why we don't do things and let ourselves believe our own excuses. Another reason, last but definitely not least and which is most relevant to this chapter, is that we always believe we have more time than we actually do. Just think if we did everything we needed to do and wanted to do RIGHT NOW, we would get so much done in life we wouldn't believe it ourselves.

The best life-lesson I took away from college was time-management skills. Between me being a full-time student with the course load, football, service to my fraternity, and my social life as well, I had to become a master of time management and priorities and that I did; not saying there isn't any room left for improvement because I can always get better. Learning to manage my time properly and juggle different things in college was a skill that I took with me into the real world after college and that little thing itself has helped me tremendously. It has allowed me to be more productive than I ever could've been had I not had the experience from college. It taught me to always keep my priorities in order. In college, they were in the order from most important to least important: 1. Academics. 2. Football. 3. Service to my Fraternity (Alpha Phi Alpha Fraternity Inc.). 4. Social life. This enabled me for after college and gave me what I needed to work 4 different jobs at once and give great effort in all of them simultaneously; it also taught me great balance.

When I use the words "most important to least important", that does not mean that one gets less effort than the other, it just means one comes before the other. They all get the same amount of effort because anything worth doing is worth over doing and if anything matters, then everything does. Let's just say, if we didn't think we could take advantage of time, we wouldn't. I'll give an example. If we say we want to be an author and we're going to write a book but we always look for "good" reasons (excuses) not to start and finish it. "I'm too young," "I don't know enough to write about," "I'll wait for the right opportunity," "I have to let the ideas come to me," "I don't know anything about editing, publishing, copyrights etc." the list goes on but you get my point. If we believe these all to be true and good reasons for our procrastination, then it will be okay in our mind to accept them.

The fact of the matter is that we only believe these excuses because we feel we have time later to write a book but the truth is, like I said earlier, we don't know how much time we actually have left on this earth. Now, I'm not naive enough to sit here and say if you do procrastinate, that you still can't and won't end up being a great author or anything else, because it's never too late to start. What I am saying is that if we didn't procrastinate as much and instead chased our dreams RIGHT NOW, we would never know how much more we could actually accomplish and how fast we could get it done. The only thing in life we cannot replace is time; it's the most precious commodity. They don't sell it in the stores and we don't have much of it to begin with; life is very short here on this earth and we're here for a great time not a long time.

We like to justify things, as I've said earlier, and we also like to compare ourselves to others. We may feel that since every New York Times best-selling author was at least over the age of 40 years (example not a researched fact) old, we subconsciously or consciously plant in our minds that we at least will be the same age to become a best-selling author. However, history is called history for a reason; barriers and records are meant to be broken. Mark Zuckerberg is the perfect example that age doesn't matter. He's the founder of Facebook and the youngest billionaire ever; he clearly didn't think he was too young to become an entrepreneur and a billionaire.

Let's not limit ourselves and justify our actions, or lack thereof, because of our way of thinking and just simply being lazy. It all comes down to us just assuming that we have more time in life than we think we do, when the reality of it is that we really don't know how much time we have in life. Why not play it safe and start living the life we want RIGHT NOW? This example is an extreme case of "what if" but it could also be a reality. What if you or I only lived to the age of 30 and for some strange reason we knew that we were going to die at the age of 30? How much more productive would we be? How differently would we live our daily life?

It wouldn't even compare to someone else who died at the age of 30 that didn't know they were going to die. Most of us don't see ourselves dying that young, so we believe the illusion that we'll have more time. I'm not trying to be negative but that's reality; we really don't know when the lights will go out and this life will be over. Like the Snickers slogan that says, "Why wait?" or the Nike slogan that says, "Just do it!" Each means just do it right now because there is no tomorrow; the best time and only time is right now, period.

I am so guilty of this myself (that's why I am using the word "we") and it hit me when I sent my good friend David a blog of mine and he thought it was very well-written. He knew that I wanted to write a book and he simply complimented me on the writing by saying, "You know, you should really write that book, P; I can't wait to read it." I did nothing but gave excuses; I said something along the lines of, "Yeah, man, I'm working on it but it's hard to write about one subject, you know? I just have to let the material come to me." That was me making excuses and being scared of the long, hard, grueling process of writing a book, in other words, I was scared to embrace the journey and start right now. I wasn't up for the challenge at that time and I was justifying my procrastination in a cowardly way.

After I hung up the phone with him, I was really ashamed of myself and the excuses I used and what I had just said to the point that I made a promise to myself: I would start my book right now, no matter how hard it would be or how long it would take me; I'm starting RIGHT NOW! I made a promise to myself that I would write every single day until my book was finished; David was the only person that I told about this promise and he held me account-able and I thank him for that. With that being said, no one knows when they are going to die so time has to be valued even more, not less. Saying that you only live once shouldn't be an excuse to live reckless but it should be the perfect reason to live an efficient life and have fun and enjoy the people in your life while you're still here.

Some people that have accomplished things that have never been accomplished are Albert Einstein, Malcolm X, Eric Thomas, LeBron James, Thomas Edison, Andrew Carnegie, Hill Harper, Barrack Obama, Oprah Winfrey, Les Brown, Tyrese Gibson, Maya Angelou, Frederick Douglas, Martin Luther King Jr, Napoleon Hill, Ben Carson, and the list goes on. If they were to have limited their thinking and imagination by comparing themselves to what others have or have not done, then no one would know who these great individuals are today. To base what you can do off of what someone else has or hasn't done is you literally failing to use all of your potential. God gave you a gift and a purpose that he gave no one else and your job is to first figure out what that is, then go after it with all you have RIGHT NOW even if it sounds crazy or has never been accomplished. If and when you don't do so, you are robbing yourself of your greatness and robbing the world of your gift that you're supposed to share and contribute to mankind.

By far, the worst part of that, in my opinion, is that if we do this we are wasting the blessings that God has put within us. I'm definitely guilty of this myself, like I said, that is the reason I used the example of becoming an author. I didn't discover my ability and gift of writing until I was 23 years old. Since, I can remember I've always loved quotes and loved how a few sentences could make me think so deeply and differently about life; I've always been fascinating by this. I've always been an inquisitive person but never thought of myself as a writer at all. I mean, I loved writing girls letters growing up in school but that was to only get girls, there was no passion for the writing itself; now that I look back, it was clear that I was gifted with words. People close to me have always told me I'm a deep thinker and a philosopher in my own way but I honestly never thought much of it; I was just simply being me.

I've always been curious about everything and questioned everything, I was big on questions not answers; I like to know "why". I also loved to read. I could read every day all day and little did I know, years and years of reading books was preparing me to become a writer. Subconsciously, I had no idea, I just liked to read because it was fun to me; it made me think and let my imagination run wild. How I came along to discover I was a writer was so ironic because it came along with giving up the thing I loved the most in life and that was football. My temporary defeat in football allowed me to discover my gift to write; like the great Eric Thomas says, "I failed forward."

The time to start is always right now because time is forever ticking no matter your circumstance. We have enough time in life to not have to rush to the point we're anxious and not enjoying the moment but we must always remember that we do not have time to waste because we don't know how much time we actually have. START TODAY AND RIGHT NOW!

# ADVANTAGES OF ADVERSITY

*"Many people have found opportunities in failure and adversity that they could not recognize in more favorable circumstances."*

*- Napoleon Hill*

Your greatest advantage is being you; using what you've been through to get to where you are going. I think as humans, we don't fully understand the power of our temporary failures and experiences. What we see as embarrassing can be our greatest strength that drives us to greatness. No one has your struggle, so that also means that no one has your motivation for the same exact reason that you do; this makes you special. Nothing is more important than the reason why you do what you do. Why you do what you do can either make you a failure or a success because that reason will either be enough to never quit or it will just be something that doesn't mean a lot to you.

You ever played on a sports team with someone who was just happy to be a part of the team and that's enough for them? Are they not the most annoying people ever? I'm sure we all have been around these types of people at some point in our lives; these are the type of people who are okay with being average. Why they're doing it isn't an extreme enough reason to be the best they can be. I'm not talking about people who don't play because they don't have enough talent but they still work their butts off; I have respect for them and their passion.

Someone playing a sport may be the only way they can possibly feed their family one day if they make it to play at a professional level, so their reason for doing what they're doing is going to be on a totally different level than others. They may have grown up in poverty and they're tired of it, so they feel a way to feed their family is through that sport they're playing. You tell me who's going to be more dangerous in their sport? This is why college players play so much harder than the professionals when it comes to sports. It goes without saying all based on what drives them; that's not just in sports but this analogy can be applied to anything in life.

If you want to know how great someone is going to be, just figure out what drives them and what they have riding on it; this will tell you everything that you need to know. How do you feel about your job that you go to everyday? Are you doing it just for the paycheck and just to keep the bills paid? Do you really have a passion for what you do and are you enthusiastic about going to work? If not, then you are not living your passion and it's time that you start to pursue it. If you don't know what your passion is, you might want to figure out what that is sooner than later.

Speaking from personal experience, my greatest failure was my greatest success. You may be wondering what does that even mean and I'll explain. My greatest failure was the best thing that ever happened to me. It brought me closer to my greatest success thus far in my life, more than any success could have. This temporary defeat was life changing for me and it had me at a low point in my life to where the only direction I could go from there was up. This is what a lot of people don't realize when they're experiencing temporary defeat in life; as long as you don't give up, the only way to go is up.

AS LONG AS YOU DON'T GIVE UP THE ONLY WAY TO GO IS UP.

I'm not going to sit up here and act like it's not easier said than done because this was the greatest challenge I've ever faced in my life and at times I didn't know if I was going to make it through. However, by the grace and strength from The Lord himself, I just kept pushing. I had been playing football since I was about 8 years old all the way up until I was about 23 years old; it was more than just a sport to me. "Football isn't life but life is football." I heard this quote somewhere and I couldn't agree with it more because football taught me everything I needed to know about life and being a man without me even realizing it. Football was a father, a girlfriend, a mentor, and anything else you can think of. When you do something for so long it just becomes a part of you and you really can't grasp the concept of life without it, so you never really prepare for that moment or day that may come; sort of like a divorce. Not to mention when a lot of people know you as "Peris, who plays football," that doesn't help the situation either.

No matter how hard we try to tell ourselves we don't, we all do to some extent, care what others think of us; especially, the important people in our lives. Out of all things in the world to fail at, I failed at the thing I loved the most and that was football. After three years of trying as hard as I possibly could to get to the NFL and being cut from a professional indoor football team, as well as a Canadian football team, I don't know why but the desire left my heart to continue playing football.

I can't explain the feeling but it was very sudden and not something I was coping with well at all. It took me awhile to come to grips with this because I didn't know what was actually happening to me, so I continued to train but my heart was not in it. Let me tell you something, I don't care what your dreams or goals are, if you're heart isn't in it then don't do it. Success in anything is too hard to reach and it's not worth it if you're not happy while doing it. I knew this at the time but I just didn't know why I was feeling this way. I didn't want to let people down and I didn't know what was next for me, which is what scared me the most of all about the situation. I always had a love and passion for football that kept me excited every day about life; the training, the good, the bad, the injuries, and everything else about it kept me going. Not to mention my girlfriend, who I thought would eventually become my wife, ended our relationship around the time so I had hit rock bottom. I had nothing to direct all of my energy and passion toward anymore.

This adversity really defined me and my character and what was about to come next in my life. I really had no one to talk to except God during this dark time in my life because I felt no one else would, or could, understand at this point. Between talking to God and starting to write down my feelings, I discovered a few things: 1. My gift to write and inspire others. 2. The most important relationship is with God. 3. I am responsible for my own happiness. These were the three things that I learned from my greatest temporary defeat in my life and those were the best lessons ever learned that

I still live by today. I had found another purpose in life; I started to put God first and I realized the key to my joy and happiness no matter the situation.

Learning that by simply having an attitude of gratitude alone, I could be happy 365 days of the year. It doesn't matter what happens to me, what someone does to me, or what life throws at me, I control my own happiness because it's how I react to things and not what happens to me. If I would have never failed, I may never have learned these key lessons about life. The part that's even better was that after learning these lessons, God put it in my heart to spread what I've learned to everyone else in the world. I was blessed and it was my responsibility to share my blessings with everyone else through speaking, writing, and building relationships with others about what I had experienced. This was my purpose in life, to spread happiness and show people that no matter where they were in life or what they had, they could make the best of their situation and have joy on the way wherever they may be going.

After giving up football and accepting that I no longer had the passion for it, I had worked numerous jobs. I worked for the Big Brother Program mentoring the youth, coached high school football, worked on the line at the Chrysler Assembly Complex building Jeeps as I stated earlier, worked with mentally disabled clients, and did substitute teaching for Toledo Public Schools as well. In the midst of all of this, life was good. I discovered my calling to write, speak, influence the world, and leave it in a better state than it was when I was born. From the outside looking in, it may have looked like a humbling experience from the chance of making it to the NFL to working a handful of part-time jobs but I knew my current situation wasn't permanent and I enjoyed what I was doing, so I didn't see it that way.

After all of this, God showed me something else and had another purpose on top of those for my life. He put the desire in my heart to become a Toledo Firefighter. I played football in high school with a couple of guys who had become Toledo Firefighters and one day one of them messaged me on Facebook and asked me if I was still pursing football. He also asked that whenever I decided to stop playing, would I sit down with him and his father, who was a firefighter as well, and talk to me about becoming one. After telling him I no longer played football, I said sure I would meet with them. Understand, I never thought in a million years about becoming a firefighter but I thought it couldn't hurt to learn about it and hear what they had to say. I never knew how little I knew about exactly what a firefighter does besides the obvious: fight fires.

As they were describing the career of being a firefighter, the whole time I couldn't help but think how didn't I know this was the perfect job for me and my personality; I was literally smiling from ear to ear and was sold within 15 minutes of the conversation. I couldn't believe that the best job in the world had been right in front of me this entire time, in my city, and I didn't know it. I also had to remind myself that God's timing is perfect and it happened this way for a reason, beyond my understanding. After having lunch with them for about 4 hours, I left there knowing I was going to become a firefighter no matter how long it took me to do so. This was the summer of 2013 and I'll never forget that day because a new fire (no pun intended) was lit inside of me and I found a new passion.

My excitement and anticipation was on an all-time high after that but the process and how long it would take would be another challenge in itself. The next Civil Service test that the City of Toledo, OH would offer to take to become a firefighter wouldn't be until May 2014, almost one year later. In that year, I had been offered a full-time position at Jeep making good money with great benefits so I quit all of my other jobs, except substitute teaching, and accepted the Jeep position full-time. I was very close to not accepting the position because working as a Temporary Part Time (TPT) worker had its advantages at Jeep. I only worked Mondays, Fridays, and Saturdays and was making decent money and I was substitute teaching Tuesdays, Wednesdays, and Thursdays so it balanced out; I was doing okay financially so I couldn't complain. My plan was to just keep working that way and turn down the full-time offer when it came around because I would have more time to study for the Firefighter Civil Service Test once the study material came out.

The class I came in with at Jeep, most of them had already got offered full-time positions so I knew I was next on the list; also before that opportunity, a boss from Human Resources came down to the line one day and pulled me to the side and said, "I didn't know you had a college degree, you know we can get you upstairs in management making a lot more money?" I politely turned down the offer of potentially making six figures, which is a lot of money for a single man with no kids. When I did, he kind of looked at me like I was crazy but in my mind all I could think about was becoming a firefighter, that's all I cared about, and that was my bottom line; no amount of money could ever change that.

I knew what I wanted and no one could dangle something in front of my face that I didn't want to make me change my mind. Making that much money may have made me comfortable to living that lifestyle and lose focus on taking the firefighter test. I had already done my homework on becoming a firefighter and I knew by making the move from jeep to the fire academy I would initially take a pay cut for the first few years, so adjusting my living financially would be inevitable. I also knew that working in upper management was even more time consuming than becoming a full-time worker on the assembly line, so I knew that would take away time from studying for the Civil Service Test. Shortly after that, they came and offered me a full-time position as an assembly line worker as I knew they would, and for some reason I decided to go against my plan and say yes; something came over me and simply said why not. I would have great benefits and not have to work so many part-time jobs, not to mention I would be making more money working one job than I was working 5 simultaneously. Money isn't the biggest factor but it's definitely a factor. However, the toughest part was leaving all of the kids that I worked with from my other jobs.

After accepting the position, I really wasn't sure I made the right decision. I got put on second shift, which I was praying I didn't and my work schedule was Monday-Saturday 5pm to 330am with only Sunday off. These were the craziest hours I've ever worked in my life and the most I've ever worked; I was making good money but I was paying for every bit of it and I had no time to even spend the money that I was making to even enjoy it. Not to mention, I was put on the most difficult team in the plant as far as physically challenging goes. Main body harnesses was the job everyone wanted to stay away from; I've seen someone about to quit their job when they had to come work on our team before they even attempted to do it because of how hard they heard it was. Thank God I was able to talk that person into not quitting and at least giving it a try first.

The job was challenging but once your hands got used to it, it got a little better only my hands were always cramping and waking me up out of my sleep at night and that wasn't that much fun. I had broken my wrist in high school so plates and screws were put in to fix it during surgery but this didn't help me with that job at all.

I'm not complaining, I just didn't see myself having to go through this challenge because all I could think about was becoming a firefighter. I felt like I just could've stayed part-time and made it easier on myself to make that transition, having more time to study on top of that; but you know how that saying goes, "God gives his hardest battles to his strongest soldiers."

Back to the reason why I loved my schedule and was hesitant about accepting the full-time position at Jeep: 1. I knew I would have to quit every last one of my other jobs if I got 2nd shift (5pm-330am) which was pretty much what they were hiring us all for, not to mention that on the Wrangler side where I had came from as a TPT they worked 2 Saturdays on and one off. The full-time employees had options to take days off when us temporary part-time workers came in but on the Cherokee side, they worked Monday-Saturday, every week of the year with no TPTs to have the options for PIC days (PIC days are Mondays, Fridays, or Saturdays being your options to take off work when the Temporary Part-Time Workers come in). They literally lived at work from 5pm-330am, Monday-Saturdays so I knew balancing other jobs was not likely. This alone made me really think long and hard, but the thing I was most worried about was studying for the firefighter test I was scheduled to take on May 31, 2014.

For about almost a year, I had been anticipating taking the firefighter written examination since I had sat down and met with my high school teammate and his father and discussed the idea of me becoming a Toledo Firefighter. Like I said earlier, I had no idea and was ignorant to the fact to what being a firefighter actually entailed. Everything about being a firefighter just had my name all over it; even after sitting down with them, I prayed a lot on it and continued to do my homework about the career, talking to plenty of other firefighters as well. I had no idea that such an honorable, fun, great, and perfect job for me existed. So, with that being said and to make a long story short, becoming a firefighter was added to my long-term list of goals. From then until the test, really all I could do to get closer to that was stay in great physical shape and network with as many firefighters who would give me time to not talk but listen to them about their experiences and advise me; I certainly took full-advantage of the experience.

It was literally like I started attracting firefighters; the law of attraction is crazy because I was meeting them by the dozens, literally. I also went to the library and checked out firefighter and EMT (Emergency Medical Technician) books to study them in the meantime until I got my study packet for the actual test. I wanted to self-educate myself on the terms and knowledge that firefighters needed to know so I could be a step ahead; you can never start too early. Each firefighter has to become EMT certified to become a firefighter for the Toledo Fire Department but that's long after the civil examination; after you pass that and go through the interview, physical test, background check, et cetera. I was claiming my blessings in advance; failure was not an option for me.

I knew a month or two before the test that I was going to get the study booklet for the test and it was going to become my new bible (metaphorically speaking). I also knew that time would be of the essence during the couple months or so that I would get to study for it. The amount of time and effort I put into studying that book could be the difference between me getting the job, not getting the job, or even having to take the test again; in other words, I knew my time would be very valued and limited. Even with those multiple jobs, the schedule I currently had working all of them would allow ample time to study. I could study while I substitute taught and I could even take days off subbing because you only subbed when you wanted to. I could study while mentoring the kids if we were at the library and they were doing homework and I could even study on breaks while at Jeep because I was still part-time.

Letting my schedule and familiarity go to accept a full-time position, possibly working 6 days a week from 5pm to 330am, would present an entire new challenge itself, as far as limiting my time. The other side of the coin was that working that one job versus working multiple jobs, I would make a lot more money than all of those others combined. But honestly, as I've already stated the worse part of leaving all the other jobs would be the kids. I have a passion for working with the youth, that is just what I'm meant to do on this earth and having to leave the kids to work in a factory for 10 hours a day 6 days a week, just didn't sit right with me.

As they were hiring us full-time workers by the week, I was pondering and praying even harder about the decision I knew I was going to have to make on the spot really soon. The question was, stay as a TPT working at Chrysler only Monday, Friday and Saturdays, along with mentoring, substitute teaching, and coaching as well with a flexible schedule to study for the firefighter test when it came around in a couple months? Or accept the full-time 2nd shift position working 6 days a week from 5pm-330am and receive full-benefits while making a lot more money but leaving my passion for working with kids and having a lot less time to study for the firefighter test when it came around?

I have to admit this was one of the hardest decisions I've ever made in my life. But as cliché as it sounds, the best things to do are always the hardest and when things get difficult that means an opportunity lies within the difficult time. Napoleon Hill said, "With every adversity carries the seed of equal or greater benefit." I agree whole heartedly with this quote. I believe that God will not allow something to be taken from you or allow you to go through hard times without replacing it with a blessing but the trouble comes in when we don't allow ourselves to step back from the situation while we're in it to see such opportunities.

One thing I try to do and I still need a lot of work on is when I'm going through something, I ask myself am I focusing on God or the problem? When I do this, it puts things into perspective for me very quickly. In the situation with me ending up deciding to accept the full-time position and getting 2nd shift, which is what I dreaded to get, I have to admit that I did not accept my own advice and keep my focus on God when things got hard. It's funny how we stress about things and at the end, they always turn out okay. We can't do anything but shake our heads at ourselves, look back on the situation, and question why we even worried in the first place; the Most High has never let me down and everything always turns out okay. I've been guilty of this numerous times and this situation was no different.

On February 28th, 2014, I was working on the line as a TPT on the Jeep Wrangler side of the plant when our Union Steward came down on the line to get me and said, "Hey Peris, you ready to accept a full-time position and start making some real money?" He asked the question in such a way that it really wasn't a question; like, who would turn down a full-time position at Jeep? People would die for a career job as such. But little did he know I was really considering not taking it, I always saw working at Jeep as a blessing but it's not something I could see myself doing for 30 years of my life; I just believed I had a different calling for my life. I just couldn't match the energy this guy had while offering me this full-time position and even still, I smiled and politely said, "Yes sir." (I literally didn't know whether I was going to accept the job or not when he asked me, I just literally went with my first mind like my mother always tells me to).

As happy and confident as I may have seemed, I was very un-sure about the decision I had just made; all I kept thinking was will I get too comfortable making this good money? Will my drive to be a firefighter die down and even if it doesn't, how am I going to find time to study working so much? There were a million potential sce-narios that were running through my head and looking back on it now, I was worried about things that hadn't even happened yet; how pointless is that? I constantly preach to people to not worry about things you can't control or things that haven't happened yet and here I was being a hypocrite, sadly to say.

The irony of it all was that a childhood friend of mine (we both got hired in as TPTs together 6 months previous and he had just got hired full-time a couple weeks before me) would complain about is how hard the job was he was on and how he hated it. I'm very optimistic so I used to just always say, "Bro, it can't be that bad." When he found out I had got hired full-time, he kept saying, "I hope they put you over here with us." I used to chuckle when he said it because I love a challenge and I wasn't worried about the type of job I got in the least bit.

So after going down to sign the papers and accept the full-time position, I was told to report to the Cherokee side Monday evening for second shift 5pm-330am, Monday-Saturday; the situation I had dreaded the most to happen, but it did. To add more on top of that, I was put on the team with my friend; Trim 2 Team 1 Main body Harnesses, the hardest job in the plant that everyone tried to bid out of and when I saw my friend, Domonique, all we both could do was crack up laughing. Come to find out, I had 2 friends from high school on this team working with me so I thought that would help my transition coming into a new environment and working a new shift but they wouldn't be there for long by my side. Domonique had just got his trucking license and my other friend was moving to Atlanta the following week for another job, so I literally worked with them both for about a few weeks or so and they were gone just like that.

I was not envious that they moved on to bigger and better things but I had just wished the firefighter thing would hurry up already so I could move on to the next best thing in my life; also, because my two friends, who I was closest with in the plant, had just left. Little did I know that the people who I remained working with at Jeep, who were strangers at the time, were the ones that I would become close to and they would become my family and support me throughout this firefighter process. We never know our assignment from God in any given situation until it all pans out; I was sent over there for a reason.

The reason I was sent over there was far bigger than me and much more about just becoming a firefighter. God blessed me with the privilege to do his work and his will for others when he sent me over there. The Lord's plan was better than mine all along and I just had to get comfortable with being out of my comfort zone. I realized that it wasn't my time, I was so worried about working all of these hours and I was just so comfortable with my old schedule that I was stuck in my ways and wasn't accepting change with a positive mindset; we all know the only constant thing in life is change.

I'm not going to lie, learning those 6 jobs on that team was pretty challenging especially with being the perfectionist that I am didn't help. I had yet to work a job using my hands to literally build cars and it was numerous times when I second guessed my decision about accepting the full-time position while frustrated with learning the jobs; it was not easy at all and the firefighter test just seemed so far away that it was hard to use as motivation. I never thought about quitting but at times I felt discouraged and had to snap myself out of the funk I was in and stay optimistic and remind myself that it was only temporary.

My friends had just left for their new journeys with new jobs and all I could do was ask God, "When is my blessing coming?" Between adjusting my sleep schedule, getting used to standing up all of those hours, my hands hurting constantly, it was just a big change for me and it was really a shift in my focus and attitude that needed a change and not my situation that needed the adjustment. What I was going through, everyone else on the team had to start there as well and they seemed to still be alive. Looking back on it, I definitely could've handled the change a little better. At times I would get off work and go to the gym, my hands would be hurting so bad that I wouldn't know how I was going to begin the workout let alone finish it, but somehow I got through it; everything is mental. Once I learned the jobs, I had to have my mind elsewhere even though my body was in that factory so I literally challenged myself to read a book a week to keep my mind in a positive state and it helped me so much.

I'm not trying to sit up here and say that working full-time was all negative because it wasn't and I eventually got used to the job and it became fun. It was just very difficult for me to find the balance between starting over on another side of the plant with a new team and learning new jobs while in the back of my mind just thinking about becoming a firefighter and leaving. I'm a person that likes routine. After taking some of my own medicine and practicing what I preached, I soon realized that me working there wasn't about me and that God had a plan for me the short time I would be there as well. The best part about working there was by far the people, I worked with some amazing individuals that became lifelong friends and that was the biggest blessing of all. When you spend 60 hours a week with someone, you see them more than your family and they literally become your family. I was blessed to meet all of these great people.

Every single person knew my plan was to become a firefighter and they all supported me 100%. They prayed for me, encouraged me, asked me for updates about the process, and much more. They kept me motivated more than they would ever know and I'm so thankful for that. I needed them because the process was so long that it became discouraging at times and doubt and fear would creep in, not fear of the danger of the job but the fear of not making it through the process and getting selected.

At this point, the main thing on my mind was the Civil Service Test. We got our study booklet in April and we had about 30 days to study it before the test. I vividly remember getting off work at 330am and going downtown and sleeping in my car in front of the Headquarters of the Fire Department until it opened at 8am to get my study booklet; at one point, I even got out of my car and slept in front of the door as the time got closer. All I could think about was studying that booklet to score number one. I wanted it so badly that failure wasn't an option, even with my past history with tests. Taking tests has never been a strength of mine and for whatever reason, I've always had to study harder and longer to do even decent on tests since I can remember. I've always been great at writing papers and such but tests just made me sweat even thinking about them, so I figured getting the book first would give me a jumpstart on everyone else who was good at taking tests because I knew I needed every advantage I could get.

I also knew that thousands of people were going to be taking this test with hundreds of them already having firefighter experience and medical experience in their background or they knew someone and that would give them an advantage. Not to mention, just the year before I had taken the graduate school test, the GRE, to get accepted into graduate school and I had failed that and got denied into a Master's Program so a lot of confidence was not something I had going into this. I just simply decided that I was going to out work everyone who was smarter than me and I was going to become a firefighter no matter what it took; I felt like I controlled my own destiny and I could do it.

When we got that study booklet, I never put it down. I was only sleeping about 3-4 hours a day on average because I had no time to waste; I even made flash cards and studied at work while building Jeeps on the line. I had my co-workers quizzing me throughout the day and I was so focused that nothing else really mattered at that point in my life. I became obsessed with that book and I was not going to let anything in my control be a reason to not make it because I decided that I was going to give it my all. I would get to work an hour in a half early every day to sit in my car and study before work.

One day, I was sitting in the break area studying and my boss came up to me and asked was I studying for school. I told him no, I already graduated from college and I was studying to become a firefighter. He told me that he didn't know I had a degree and he mentioned that there were other jobs paying more that were available there that he could get me in. I humbly declined making six figures again because I knew what I wanted to do and was sticking to my plan. Again, he looked at me like I was crazy for turning down that job offer making all of that money.

People are not going to understand your dreams so don't ever expect them to and the devil is always going to test you when you want something; he'll offer you things that look appealing or look better from the outside looking in and you have to have the will power to say no to anything that isn't exactly what you want, period. You cannot settle, even if they're so close you can barely tell the difference. Like I stated earlier, I knew that if I started making six figures I might have gotten comfortable with that money and it may have been harder to study for my test or I may have lost motivation or whatever the case may have been, but I thank God till this day that I had the will power and discipline to say no.

There were also more blessings going on at Jeep; I mentioned that my working there was much bigger than me. I had a guy on my team who was an atheist and I, myself, being a believer in Christ and being very secure in that no one else's faith, religion, or lack thereof bothered me in the least bit. I don't even bring up my belief to most people because I feel they should see it through my way of living instead of me talking about it, but that's just me. I remember one day he just simply asked me why was I always so happy and inspirational about life and how did I get like that. I simply told him, "It's the God in me. He has blessed me and I just love life and want to bless others." This is before I knew he was an atheist. After giving honor to God for how happy I was, he gave me a strange almost 'I wasn't expecting you to say that look' and simply said, "This may offend you but I don't believe in God." I said, "Okay, that's fine. I was just answering your question and telling you why I'm the way that I am." That was the end of that conversation,

I had no intentions of trying to persuade him in any way and I didn't think of him any different, I just remember praying after that conversation and asking God to use me as a tool if that's what my purpose for being there was because it was going to take more than me to help guide him towards the Lord. To make a very long story short, this guy became one of my great friends and one of the people I became closest to while working at Jeep; we even still talk to this day and he also became a believer. Not because of me but

because God used me as a tool to do his work and I simply accepted that, so to God be the glory! My time spent there was definitely
not in vain and I don't regret any minute of it.

If I would've accepted any of those two offers at a higher position maybe I wouldn't have been able to have been a tool to help
my friend develop a relationship with God; who knows? So many
people inspired me to chase my dreams I'm just humbled to inspire someone else in any way, shape, or form. I also had another
great friend while working there where all we did was inspire each
other and we were always looking for new ways to grow. We both
read book after book and had debates daily, disagreements, and
you name it, he was and still is part of my mastermind circle.

At one point, we even challenged each other to work 100hrs
in one week; we worked so much over time that we barely slept. It
wasn't about the extra money but just constantly challenging each
other to get out of our comfort zone. My favorite thing that we
always discussed was our plan to get out of Jeep and how we were
going to do it. Mine was obviously becoming a fire fighter and also
becoming a published author. We both had our plans and we were
both dedicated to making our dreams a reality; nothing against
working at Jeep but we both just knew from the day we started that
there was more for us in life than working 30 years there.

After taking the test, it was a big relief but at the same time,
it added anxiety and anticipation to get the results. The results
would take 4 months to get back and it was the longest 4 months of
my life, I must say. I'll never forget the day I woke up and got those
results from that test. At first, I instantly became upset because I
didn't score number one which was my goal but then I began to
realize that over 500 people passed the test. I was in the top 100
and the number 1 scoring minority which gave me a great chance

to get picked for the first class, which was my ultimate goal so I had to shift my attitude and remain positive for the long haul because I still had a long way to go in the process.

A couple firefighters I knew had called to congratulate me on passing and getting a high score on the test so that helped and made me feel better about not scoring number one. If you set the bar high, you'll always achieve high enough to get to where you need to be. I truly believe by my goal being to score number 1, it enabled me to study as hard as I could to be number one. After the test scores were out, the FBI and BCI background checks had started. They took the top 200 scorers on the test and assigned each one a detective to conduct an extensive four month background check on their life. They talk to anyone from your neighbors, spouses, family, landlords, current and past employers, high school, and even elementary school teachers. They check criminal and driver's records, credit scores, credit card bills, and anything on your record or anything negative in your background check is used as points against you. If you get a certain number of points you're disqualified from becoming a firefighter, doesn't matter if you passed the test.

It all comes down to the fact that so many people want to become firefighters that they have to find fair and legitimate ways to eliminate people to make the selection process easier. This is what the background check, the interview, and physical ability test are all for as well as to try to judge good character as well. After going through the four month background check, you get your scores back and you have a time period to set a court date and appeal any of your points, if you will. I, myself, ended up with one point against me and I appealed it with good reason and got it erased so I went into the next step with 0 points on my background check; that was a great start. Next, was the oral interview where you sit in front of a panel of firefighters, officers, and a chief to be asked questions and answer them to the best of your ability; to some people this is the most frightening thing ever, having to speak in front of people let alone having to be scored on points to the questions asked to get the job of your dreams.

There were a series of questions they ask you and you're graded on all the points you hit or don't hit by how you answer each question. I wasn't as nervous about this as I was taking the test; I'm naturally a good speaker and people don't generally make me nervous. I figured the questions couldn't be too difficult so all I needed to do was relax and be me. I asked around as well as went on the internet to search 'commonly used firefighter interview questions' so I could practice and get prepared for this interview. Doing that research and talking to people came to be very helpful for my interview and I was relaxed while being nervous simultaneously; I felt like I knocked it out the park and I must've done well enough because I passed. My track coach always told me, "If you're not nervous, you're not ready."

The last and final part of the process to pass before the fire academy was the firefighter physical ability test. This was essentially a timed obstacle course performing a series of firefighter task while wearing firefighter personal protective equipment with a self-contained breathing apparatus. You must perform all of the tasks without making a mistake, which failing one will cause you to fail the entire test, while getting the entire thing done under a certain amount of time. I was a little worried about this because I had never done any firefighter related work up to this point and I wasn't worried about being in shape because I knew I was in good enough shape, I just didn't know how good and efficient I would be at everything we had to accomplish. The good news was that they gave us two practice sessions before the actual test day and this was very helpful; you got to go through the obstacle course and get timed and they would also coach you up on stuff you're doing wrong or could do better.

I remember the first time going through it I just went as fast as I could and I was so nervous, even though it was just practice my adrenaline was pumping good. I passed that first practice session but the second practice session I actually failed because while carrying the ladder in that part of the obstacle, I let the ladder scrape the ground which is an automatic failure. This didn't help my nerves at all going in to take the real test that actually counted. When the test came around, I felt confident but nervous at the same time. What makes it more nerve-wracking is that they don't tell you if you passed or failed right away, you have to wait a few days for your results. You can imagine how long those 3 days were for all of us.

Receiving that email saying I passed the physical ability test was one of the best days of my life; at that point I had passed everything and done all that was within my control to get closer to my goal of becoming a Toledo Firefighter. Now all I had to do was wait to see if I would be picked to be in the first class of the academy. Back in the summer of 2013 when I decided I wanted to become a firefighter, I wrote down a few things: score number one on the civil service examination, get in the first class of the academy, work the hardest, and give the best effort in the fire academy. I didn't want to wait around for the next class, I wanted to be first. With the blessing and favor from God, I received the email that I would be accepted into the 290th Fire Academy class of the Toledo Fire and Rescue Department and I would be getting sworn in to start the academy on May 29, 2015. I cried tears of joy when I read that email! All that I had prayed and worked for was coming true and the joy was a bit overwhelming.

When I gave the good news to all of my family at Jeep, they were just as happy if not happier than me that my dream was coming true; they all knew how long and how badly I had wanted it. I remember like it was yesterday, putting in my 2 week notice to my supervisor to resign from Jeep and her asking me, "You sure you want to do this? You know I can get you a job higher up making more money if you don't want to work on the line?" (Here's another offer at making six-figures.) I smiled and politely said, "Yes, I'm sure. I'm going to be a firefighter; this is what I was meant to do."

As the time wound down for me to leave Jeep, it was definitely a bitter sweet feeling. Going on to an exciting new journey that once was just a long awaited dream but leaving all the people that I worked with for two years that I had become so close with. On my last day working at Jeep, they didn't make it any easier by throwing me a surprise going away party with all kinds of good food, cake, sweets, and such. They just don't know how much that meant to me and I will forever appreciate them. I learned so much about myself and about life working there but most importantly, I learned that there's a lot of great people in this world that want to see you succeed just as bad as you do and when you're surrounded by great people, it's inevitable that you'll fall nothing short of greatness.

I've experienced, as well as observed, that people who are successful are people who just kept the same enthusiasm when they failed; they found something deep down inside of them to push them to keep going. At times you don't know where you're going or where you'll end up but I promise you that if you just keep going, God will take you to exactly where you need to be. Our job is just to not give up, keep going, and the Most High will take us to blessings that we can't even imagine. At one point I thought my life was over when football didn't work out but now I see that football all along prepared me to become the best firefighter, author, and motivational speaker I can be to serve the people. That temporary defeat made me strong enough to handle my bigger blessings that I didn't even know were in my future; to God be all the glory. Our temporary failures are not meant to hold us back and discourage us but they're meant to build upon and lift us higher than we'll ever challenge ourselves to go if we never failed.

# FIND YOUR PASSION

*"Once you find out what you want, spend the rest of your
natural life waking up, and going after it."*

*- Eric Thomas*

One day my best friend, Don, saw me state my opinion on
some topics on social networks and suggested that I start
a blog. I thought about it for a second even though I didn't really want to but I value his opinion so I said why not? I thought to
myself, it's a way to express myself and state my opinions and view-
point on things which I love to do, not to mention it would be very
therapeutic for me. More importantly, it allowed me to help and
inspire people with my gift of words.

After writing my first few blogs, I gained confidence quickly;
I knew they were good because of the zone I would get in when
I would write them. Also, when I finally worked up the guts to
share them with others, I got all positive feedback. People said how

much my writings helped and inspired them, and they could relate to everything I wrote. When people started saying these things and the feeling it gave me, I knew right then and there that a writer is what I wanted to be and I realized it was a gift; I had to use it to bless others because that's what God wanted.

Back to the zone I would get in when I would write, it made me aware that my writings were not just me and were much bigger and more intellect than I possessed. Some people call them "hutches," "energy," "the universe," "infinite intelligence," "your subconscious," "Holy Spirit," and the list goes on. All I know is that the power does exist that's bigger than us and the finite intellectual brain that we possess. When I would write these ideas, words, or messages would just come in flashes without much effort or thinking being done. They would come at random and weird, inconvenient times; mostly, real late at night around two in the morning or so.

I could kind of feel when it was about to happen because I would lay down for bed around 11pm or so and at times I would even be extremely tired but no matter what, I just couldn't fall asleep. So after a few hours of just lying in my bed in the dark, I would get my computer out and just begin writing; it was like me outside of myself and something greater replacing me taking over my actions. The feeling was so pure and I was so conscious in the moment that I know that God was present and working through me with the Holy Spirit and all around me as a tool to bless others.

As I've stated earlier, I discovered my gift of writing when I was 23 years old and decided I wanted to write a book. I'm not going to say I wasted a handful of years of my life but I definitely wasn't as productive as I could've been from then until now writing this. At the time, I wasn't taking my own advice that I'm giving you in this book that the only time is RIGHT NOW! When I first announced, which was actually on Facebook, that I was going to write a book, I got again nothing but encouragement and positive feedback and I was motivated more than ever. Eventually, that new "exciting" feeling goes away and the real challenges begin. This is the time when life tests you to see how bad you really want something.

When at times I would want to write, I couldn't find that "supernatural" energy that I felt I once possessed to work on my book and it felt like when I didn't have that, my writings were average and I was forcing it. It made me not feel like writing unless I felt like writing, if that makes sense. I started thinking things like I'm young, I have my whole life to write a book, and to even experience more things so I would actually have something to write about because I'm so young. I remember my friend, David, was reading one of my blogs I had sent to him and was moved by it and he texted me and said, "P, you should write a book seriously, man." I remember responding by saying something like, "Yea, I'm actually going to but it's hard to focus on one subject to write an entire book. My mind wanders and it makes it very hard to write so I know it will come with time." When I said this to him, at the time it seemed like a perfectly logical explanation, right? After a week or two went by, it hit me that I gave excuses; all reasons why I couldn't write my book RIGHT NOW instead of reasons why I can and should.

I'm here to tell you that whatever your passion is you will not always feel like practicing your craft. If you want to be great, it takes a lot of practice (10,000 quality hours is what studies says it takes to reach mastery), failure, criticism, self-doubt, and mental blocks; in other words, a lot of bad before the good. I was scared of failure and being mediocre but at the same time, I was increasing my chances of mediocracy by only writing when I felt like it and in the spirit to do so. The formula is really simple in life, if you want to be a great basketball player, then you practice basketball all the time. Football: practice football, lift weights, and watch films all year around, not just when you feel like it or when the coach tells you to. This goes for any profession; actors, boxers, doctors, lawyers, the list is infinite and it goes for any and everything. This doesn't mean practicing when you feel like it or only when you feel good or confident in yourself about your abilities; when you don't feel like it, someone else does so you'll end up getting left behind.

I'm sure we've all heard the quote, "You either get better or worse," and I stated earlier that by me not writing on a consistent basis and working on mastering my craft, not only were others getting ahead of me but I was prolonging my success and greatness. Now, I do agree with that saying but I'm not sure we all understand it. We don't actually get worse when we don't practice, we stay the same but other people get better that we're in competition with. When we meet up with them in some form or fashion, they will outperform us and take an opportunity that we were not prepared for due to lack of practice; it's very difficult to perform what you don't practice. In reality, we just stayed the same.

Think back when you were in elementary school or even junior high and it was that one athlete who was a physical specimen and his or her skills were just way more advanced than everyone else's. You probably thought, "Wow! This person is going to college on a scholarship." But what happened when you all got to high school? The competition, including you, caught up with that person's talent. Them being so good, successful, being praised and talented at a young age caused them to be complacent. Since day one, they've always been naturally better than everyone so they've never been motivated to practice to keep getting better. If you're not getting better, someone else is. There are no short cuts to greatness, it takes constant hard work and the time is always RIGHT NOW to do so.

You may be thinking, "Well, I've seen people not put in the hard work in high school and get a college scholarship", well I'm here to tell you that all bad habits eventually catch up to you and they will be exposed. The day will come and they will have to make a choice to either just ride their pure talent and get by or put in the work necessary to become great and help the team and themselves to reach their full potential. If you take short-cuts, you'll always get cut short; that's just the rules to life. They either adapt to what it takes, put in the hard work, and practice their craft as if their life depended on it or they skate by and become one of the people who live with regret, always talking about the past and how good they "used to be." I'm sure we all know some of these people; I've seen both case scenarios first-hand.

I said all that to say this: that was me and my procrastination about writing. I was fearful of failing and having to grind it out, being a good writer to working constantly hard to become great. The transition from good to great in anything is very difficult and uncomfortable. I don't even like the word "good" anymore, I refuse to use it; I literally say "great morning" and "great night". You can ask anyone that knows me that I don't use the word and I want greatness in everything with my name on it. When this hit me that I was making excuses, I called my friend, David, back and told him so and I said, "No, I'm writing my book now. I'm going to practice writing every day whether I feel like it or not until my book is complete." I made a vow that the only way I can get better at writing is by writing. I don't know what it takes to be a great writer but I know it's not accepting being a good writer; to be great, you have to put being good at risk. I know I'm going to be great no matter how long it takes but the time it takes will be as short as it can possibly be from a time stand point because I'm starting RIGHT NOW so procrastination will not play a part.

To sum this chapter up, when you have a problem or goal to accomplish, we're either doing one of two things: we're either finding ways or reasons (excuses) to procrastinate on working toward the goal and focusing on the problem instead of the solution or we are using the time RIGHT NOW to find any and every reason to reach our goal or deal with the problem to find the solution. Just think about it, it's impossible to complain or procrastinate and move forward and get better simultaneously. If we complain about something and we have it in our control to do something about it, we are literally wasting time. To the contrary, if we are complaining or worried about something we cannot control, we are wasting our time as well. We have to learn to use our RIGHT NOW and todays more wisely; not sometimes when we feel like it but all the time so we can reach our full-potential.

I used to highly dislike and take offense growing up when I played sports when my coach or anyone would say, "Peris, you have a lot of potential." I know it's a good thing and it's meant to encourage but I always believed potential meant absolutely nothing, what about my RIGHT NOW. What am I doing wrong or right RIGHT NOW to help me reach or not reach my full-potential, is what I wanted to know. I was more concerned and focused on my present and who and what I was at the time, not who and what I wasn't in the future; I have no idea why this offended me as a kid.

What I am talking about is taking advantage and working on the present is the only way we can reach our full potential. In other words, if you tell someone they have the potential to be successful, tell them things they can do RIGHT NOW to get there. Otherwise, it's a pointless statement to make. How we use our RIGHT NOW is a reflection of what we've. 1. Learned from our past. 2. Where we will be in the future. Focusing on anything besides the RIGHT NOW is either keeping you in your past or dwelling on the future which hasn't happened yet.

Now, some may ask what if they are focusing on a positive past? Well that can be good to an extent, but focusing on past accomplishments can breed complacency. The only thing harder than becoming successful is staying successful. Once you feel you've made it to the top it's natural for us to stop working as hard as we did to get there; that's human nature. We have to want to get better on purpose and have to fight against ourselves to want to relax because we feel we've "made it". Of course, it starts with you but that's the importance of keeping people around you who will always keep you grounded and challenged. Beware of "yes men" and "ego strokers" in your circle. It's only human nature when you hear enough good about yourself that you will start to believe it.

I always like to say beware of the two C's: compliments and criticism. They both carry the same tools of destruction just in two different forms. Only listen to either one when necessary. It's like our groups of friends we have, we all know when to call which one based on what we want to hear when we have an issue. We know which friend to call that will let us have a pity party for ourselves and they'll usually join in. We know which friend to call to always give us positive feedback and look at the bright side of things who'll never allow a pity party. We have the friend who's a little bit of both. We also have the friend who has no filter or bias and will always tell you how it is whether you like it or not; this is a great friend that's showing you tough love, keep them around. We all know which to call based on our mood and feelings and situations whether we want to focus on the problem or solution or whether we just want to vent or fix the problem.

All of these types of friends are necessary to an extent just like compliments and criticisms are both necessary to a certain extent. I know me and I'm the friend who's going to be positive with no bias and all of my friends know this about me. I'm going to tell them how it is whether they like it or not and I'm going to seek the positive out of every situation, so calling me is not a good idea if you're not ready to work toward the solution. They know when to call me and know what to expect based on their present feelings about their situation. This doesn't make me a better friend or a better person than the pity party friend; it just makes us different with different roles.

As much as I highly dislike saying this, we all, including me, need empathy at times (in moderation of course) and just need to vent from time to time. I've been called "too positive" or "insensitive" for not being that other type of friend but I personally don't care because that's not me; I cannot be anyone but me and that's all you'll ever get. I'm just naturally all about being positive and moving forward; I want to get from A to B as fast as I can if A is not where I want to be. If I were to be anything else other than who I am and tell you something I don't feel, wouldn't tell, or allow myself to do then I'm being a disservice to you. God made me and who I am is the person I'm evolving into every day for a reason and you also. So be who you are and be that 100% of the time in the RIGHT NOW; nothing more nothing less and people will have no choice but to respect and appreciate you for it.

# HELPING OTHERS

*"Humility is the bedrock security that doesn't de-
mand or expect applause or recognition. The essence
of genuine humility isn't thinking less of ourselves
but thinking of ourselves less."*

*- Samuel Chand*

Helping others is something I realized I was good at a very
long time ago. It was something that came naturally and
something I just loved doing because of the feeling it brought
me; more importantly, the feeling it brought to those who I
would help. In my personal opinion, there's no greater feeling
in the world than to help someone and love someone. It didn't
take me long to figure out not only was I good at helping others but little did I know it was my calling in life; in other words,
it's one reason God created me and put me on this earth. No
different than Michael Jordan being blessed and gifted to play
the game of basketball because that's what he was built for. He

was built to play the game of basketball and entertain the sports world; but in my opinion, more importantly, he was meant to inspire kids and millions of people all over the world to chase their dreams with a determination that the world cannot deny you if you persevere.

With that being said, just because you're naturally good at something by no means does that mean it will be an easy road and that you will not face challenges. Michael Jordan, for instance, got cut from his high school basketball team as a sophomore. We all know how competitive MJ was about everything, especially, basketball so we can only imagine the feeling of devastation when he found out he hadn't made the team. It was one or two ways he could've handled that situation: he could've felt sorry for himself and gave up which we for sure wouldn't be talking about MJ like we do today or he could've used him getting cut as motivation to prove to himself, not others, that he was destined for greatness. His story in itself is an inspiration for anyone who wants to achieve anything; whether it's sports related or not. He's the all-time winner and has the never give-up attitude, in my opinion, and his drive helped others.

My way of helping others is a little different than playing professional basketball, winning multiple championships, and selling the same shoes over and over. I was fortunate enough to go to college and play football on a scholarship at Miami University and had the greatest time of my life learning so much about myself while growing into the man I am today. Getting a top notch education from one of the best schools in the country and not to mention competing against the best athletes in the world in division I college football and even winning a championship along the way, that was a blessing in itself and I know for a fact it inspired kids back home to do the same and chase their dreams.

I know this because they've told me so and that was better than the experience because it lets you know that people look up to you and your blessings and success reach people when you don't even realize it; it's a very humbling experience and words cannot express the feeling of gratitude it brings.

With that being said, I know that football window for myself was very short when it was all said and done and I definitely enjoyed it while it lasted. I am in no way downplaying that blessing because I still hear from people how my career inspired them and it's a lovely thing but over time between the transition of me being done with football and moving on to the next chapter in my life, I discovered a new blessing within me to help others in an entirely different way. It's so funny how things work out because it's like everything was perfect timing. Little did I know, as my football career was winding down and my heart's desire was soon about to change, I discovered the love for words and writing and as I stated in the last chapter with encouragement from a friend I decided to take it seriously

In my eyes I had no idea this was going to come about; I was so focused and had such tunnel vision on making it to the NFL that no one in the world could tell me anything different. I was really starting to get a lot of attention as far as social media about how inspiring my tweets and Facebook posts were very inspiring and thought it was something that could be taken to another level. And it's quite ironic because as I would post motivating Facebook posts and tweets on Twitter, a lot of it was to get myself inspired for the numerous workouts I had for the upcoming day to train for the NFL; it was kind of like motivating myself. As time passed, I came to find out as I was motivating myself, I was also motivating others and I'm here to tell you that helping others is a better feeling than helping yourself by far.

I know this was nothing but the work of God because I never thought I was an above average writer, even though I did like writing in my High School English class in high school (my favorite and having the best teacher in the world, Mrs. Peters, didn't hurt either) and college but I just think I preferred writing papers versus tests because tests were not my strength by any means. I always thought studying for a test and memorizing information to regurgitate it all for a test was stupid and it just simply means some people memorize better than others but when you write, you can express who you are and that, in itself, is intelligence to me. I also know that God put it in my friend, Don, to reach out and give me a push to start writing to inspire others because had that come from someone else besides Don, which it had before, I would not have been motivated to actually attempt it.

It took for my best friend to give me that push and say that to me to even really believe that he was sincere about it and for me to not be stubborn to even entertain his suggestion, let alone even take action. In my eyes God knew the plan all along but to me, as I look back on it, it's kind of funny how it worked out perfectly and I got out of my own way. At times we really can be our biggest obstacles to blocking our own blessings.

After that suggestion, I basically started a blog and never looked back. I started the blog with poems and they transferred me into doing inspirational messages on social networks every morning into writing this book. I had no idea that God had blessed me with words and the spirit and capability to inspire people the way that he is allowing me to.

I would get all kinds of messages from people I knew and people I've never met in my life about how inspiring and helpful my morning posts and my writings had been to others and it is a very humbling thing to hear. I was really blown away when I would hear these things; it was beyond me. I always tell people my inspirations are beyond me, it's a higher power (God) because this was nothing I never practiced or ever was interested in but it all just worked out that way. I never even entertained the thought of having to do something else besides playing football as a professional until my career ended. Not that I couldn't do anything else; I had my degree so I was good there, in my mind I just wasn't going to have to find a regular job until after football, meaning after a long career and then retiring.

Discovering writing and the desire to become a firefighter may have been the best things that ever happened to me for that transition in my life. You can say I had all my eggs in one basket but I like to say, "I had all my eggs in one basket and kept close watch on that basket." So in a sense, I didn't have a plan B; my plan B was to make plan A work and I do not regret that mindset because it's who I am. It was my ambition and desire that drove me and how hard I worked, I will NEVER regret all the time I put into that because it made me who I am today.

Never in a million years would I have thought that something else like writing, inspiring, and becoming a firefighter could drive me to have the same passion, ambition, and motivation that football brought me. Football and writing are very different; they by no means bring the same feeling. Football was a team sport but you still have to be individually driven, while writing for me at least is all about serving others; they are the two things I can easily put my everything into, even my emotions, and be okay with it. It's like the two things felt so right and they make me feel it's okay to be me and I could be anything I want to be when I was playing football or writing. I can't stress how much I thought that nothing else besides football would bring me that feeling; all the athletes out there know what I'm talking about.

I say sports because sports are in its own category when it comes to careers and such. Some people think they're over paid, spoiled, and the list goes on. I'm not here to argue any of that because I know if you were an athlete, you wouldn't say those things because you would understand and wouldn't say it in the first place. Sports are different in the most obvious way since you cannot play them forever; writing is something I can do until the day that I die, literally, and that idea alone is very exciting to me. It's not the same for sports though.

In sports, whether you have a professional career or not, your window is very small and athletes tend to think (even though we actually know better) that we can play forever. It's not arrogance or an invincible feeling, it's just that you simply cannot imagine life without that sport because you've played it all of your life; it's a love that cannot be explained. No matter if you play 5 years as an athlete or 20, you'll never be satisfied or ready to leave the game. The game a lot of times is why you are the man or woman you are today in a good way, it developed you not just as an athlete but an individual and it gave you character.

Little did I know that I could give everything in me to writing, inspiring, and helping others just like I did in football without ever second guessing it and I thank God for directing that passion, desire, motivation, and eagerness to something else when my football window closed; when it did and my passion began to shift, I literally didn't know what to do. When that window closes as an athlete, especially, when it's unexpected, you're in shock, denial, and some people even become depressed; it's a difficult thing to deal with and I know from personal experience. I am a firm believer that

ALL things work together for a greater cause that we may not be able to see yet or even imagine in our wildest dreams. My story here is proof because I will explain how football (even though I didn't go to the NFL but the experience from playing in college and training for the NFL) set the foundation for the rest of my life.

This book and my writing and being a motivational speaker would not have been possible without football and I truly believe that is a fact. I never looked at writing or football as something I was just doing like a hobby or just for fun (even though they both are fun to me), it was just me being me and who I was; it was an expression or an extension of me, for lack of better terms. You may be thinking that is deep and football or anything shouldn't define who you are as a person but for me during the moment in those seasons of my life they did define me.

Football and writing isn't work for me; it's too hard to be just work, if it only felt like work and I was only doing it for money, my motivation would not have withstood the long journey. When love is involved it makes work feel like play and that's what football and writing is to me; it's play time. I have fun with it, commit countless hours to it, and put everything I have into it and at the end of the day, the results don't matter how they fall into place because I only know how to give my all and that's what I did every single day.

I have never known anyone to regret putting their all in something, people only regret when they don't give something everything they have but the only way you can invest everything you have into something is if you really love it. Football and sports in general are the first things I would ever put 100% into and not second guess it. I was always skeptical of putting my all into other people because people have motives, not all but some and I couldn't and didn't want to deal with being left with the short end of the stick. So I guess you can say I over compensated in other areas of my life in things such as football and sports in general. No injury or setback of any kind could ever discourage me from playing or working hard at it; honestly, those types of things motivated me to work even harder when I would be allowed to play again after a serious injury. I never thought that certain body parts would never work the same again or I could hurt myself again; I didn't care about those things because I was the ultimate optimist when it came to the game of football.

*"An optimist sees the opportunity in every difficulty."*

*- Winston Churchill*

All these things that I gave of myself in football and the things that it gave and taught me, little did I know I would need all of these things to become everything else I wanted to be for the remainder of my life; whether it was becoming an author, motivational speaker, firefighter, or just a successful man in life in general to be a positive example that others could look up to. This is what I mean when I say all things work together for the greater good. I could start from the simple disciplines that football taught me from punctuality, hard work, putting the team before myself, commitment, perseverance, and the list continues. These things have helped me to remain positive and make the best of everything I have because football taught me if you work really hard and keep working really hard no matter what, the results will ALWAYS pay off. It may not be when you want it to or what you want it to be or expect it to be but it will pay off and that correlates to any and everything else in life I've learned.

I've learned and I am still learning that everything you do in life will be a challenge no matter what; there really is no easy way out. Quitting is easy, yes, but it's still hard to live with quitting so, therefore, quitting in itself is hard; not giving up is just harder that's all. That, in itself, is why there are more people average at what they do versus great at what they do because they simply don't want to put in the time or effort. Some people are okay with being average and that's fine as long as you can live with that. Every choice has its consequences and accepting being average usually has negative consequences. You may taste success and it may not last but being successful, means just being happy and not having much to complain about, especially, when you realize you live a life that has more blessings to be thankful for than problems to complain about.

I'm learning that those type of people put 100% into whatever they do; they're always trying to get better and they are usually overall positive people. Most successful people are harder on themselves than they are on others and that's okay, I can totally relate because who knows your potential and believes in you more than you? The answer is no one so you should be your own worse critic. At some point in your life, everyone will critique you and at another point, everyone will congratulate you and you need not listen to either because one will cause you to doubt yourself and the other will cause you to believe how good you are. That's why I've never listened to people when they say, "you're too hard on yourself", I just don't believe in that; expecting perfection of yourself is one thing and unrealistic but expecting greatness is another and definitely is an attainable goal.

After realizing that I was good at helping people and knowing that it came naturally to me, it was something I just simply loved doing at all times. It also taught me things about myself that I had to learn and unlearn just so I could become better at helping others. The thing about helping others is that it's an ongoing process and the more you help others, the more you have to change and constantly learn and unlearn. I've learned that helping others can no way, shape, or form be about you! When you're helping someone, you are not relevant. Now, I know people say if you can't help yourself then you cannot help others and I completely agree. If you haven't already helped yourself, you shouldn't be helping others anyway and if you think helping others will bring you good karma, then you're not helping others genuinely and you have an ulterior motive; it's about you not the person you're helping.

My mindset and the foundation I've built I became mature in my beliefs, which took quite some time. I came to learn that God has me and I will never live in want or need so I was sent here to help others and that's what I'm blessed to do. Quite the contrary, we all need help or an ear to listen or whatever from time to time because we're all human; we should never be too proud to ask for that shoulder to lean on when necessary and I've been blessed enough to have a family and great friends that's there at any time when I need that. The saying, "What does the person do who always helps people when they need help", is a quote I highly dislike; if you need help, you ask for it. Don't pity yourself because you're always helping people and don't expect people to help the way you do, they're not you. It's not the people's fault that you're too proud to ask for help, the fact that you feel you need to play the role as superman or woman rests with you.

This is why helping people can be very taxing on you if you're not careful because it's easy to get caught up to think that you have to be there for everyone and fix everything, which should not be the case and if it is, then you need to reevaluate yourself. If you're not okay then get yourself together before you try to help others, people you help will respect you more for this; it will allow them to relate with you more versus them maybe feeling inferior to you because they're always coming to you for advice; they have to know that you're human, too.

The key to helping others is to already be helped and together yourself, not perfect but if you have an issue deal with it because otherwise you cannot help someone else to the best of your ability. That's why I say it cannot be about you, you have to already be out of the way and give your full attention, listening to the one in need. This is a lot easier said than done because, like I said, when you're that person that everyone comes to, you start to feel obligated to be there for people and you sometimes without you even realizing it start to put yourself second. You should always be first; I'll say that again, YOU SHOULD ALWAYS BE FIRST!!

In my opinion, God's love and self-love are the most important loves because if you don't have those two then you simply cannot love someone else no matter what; it just will not work and it'll eventually catch up to you. Helping, loving, and inspiring is just giving your all to someone and doing everything you possibly can to help that individual for the better of them. Sometimes, that means not helping someone. That constantly helping someone can actually cripple them and you can be a safety net for that person; they will never learn or get stronger if you never let them fall. I know this is easier said than done but this type of help is what I find to be the hardest. Believe me, that person may thank you later or they may never thank you at all but you've actually helped them by not helping them.

A perfect way to find out if you're helping someone or crippling them by helping them too much is by the first time you refuse to help them and how they respond. If they respond negatively and forget everything you've already done, then there you have your answer; they became to expect you to help them and you're not actually helping them and never was in the first place. There is also no need to name off a list of all the things you've helped them with either because obviously that didn't mean anything to them so just save your breath.

I read the book titled "Road Less Traveled" by Scott Peck and it talks about how listening takes effort and it's more exhausting than people realize; people fail to realize that we are all not as good of listeners as we like to think we are. He says that most people listen not to listen but listen and simultaneously think what to respond with next versus actually digesting what the other person is saying. I couldn't agree more because I am too guilty of it myself and most of the time what you end up saying is about you and not them. Just think about it how many times you use a relevant story of yourself when it's something similar to their situation. It's not that you mean any harm but we simply like to talk about ourselves, that's just the way we are.

I challenge you to try this out, you can do it with a complete stranger you just met or a good friend or family member you have. Just while you're having a general conversation, find something that peaks their interest and something they can 100% relate to or they love or feel like they're an expert in. Bring up this topic and ask tons of questions while showing genuine interest and curiosity and watch how little you talk and how much they talk and constantly talk about themselves; it's like you're not even there anymore. Even when you do say something, they won't acknowledge it or they'll automatically use what you said to continue talking about themselves. Trust me, this works about 99% of the time for me and I at times have to hold my laugh in because it amazes me how selfish we can be.

Now, if the opposite happens and they ask what you think and actually listen to what you say, that simply means the person is genuinely interested in you and they're a good listener. There are some good listeners out there, they're hard to find but there are some. I've learned that if you really want to help someone then you have to be a good listener. Listening is hard; it takes self-control and a ton of concentration because when most people are in need of help, they want to vent and not always receive a solution to their problem. Us being so called helpers and good listeners, we want to counter everything they say because we assume that their thinking may not be logical but we're actually not listening to them because when people are venting, you listening is what may actually help them; not you talking or responding. It's a time and place for everything but we want to help people how we want to help people and, like I said earlier, helping people cannot be about you for you to be a great helper.

Just because you're a good helper who people come to for help, doesn't mean they want to hear what you have to say when you want to say it; it's not that simple people are more complex than that. Different things are needed at different times for different individuals because all individuals are not the same. You'll get tired of me saying this in this chapter but you have to take yourself out of the equation when you're helping others.

I'll use a baby for an example, I'm not a father so I'm writing this from experience with babies and talking to parents. I learned something that was to me quite astounding. I was told by many parents that babies have different types of cries. When I first heard this, I was thinking how is that possible but little did I know it actually made a lot of sense once it was explained to me. You'll soon understand if you already don't, but babies have different cries for when they're hungry, wet, sleepy, need to be burped, or just want to be picked up. After people told me this, I made the observations that it was definitely true and I was so amazed. What's even more amazing is that all mothers can even tell the difference between all of the types of cries. The point is that babies have different needs and they cry out different ways depending on which need they seek to be met.

What are toddlers, teenagers, and adults? They're all just older babies, correct? When we grow older, we all still have needs and wants for the same and different reasons but we want what we want when we want it. So as adults, we cry tears like babies do sometimes but for the most part our cries also become different as well for different things; it may not be a literal tear cry but we cry out for help just as much as babies. Where it gets tricky for helpers is not for them to help these different cries but first to differentiate the cries to which cry means what. This is where we have to take ourselves out of the equations as a helper. If you attempt to feed a baby when their cry is because they're wet and needs to be changed then you're going to still have a crying baby crying for what it really wants. There's no difference with adults; that's why listening is a skill and is so vital and taking yourself out of the equation is mandatory.

As a parent, if the baby is crying and you're just annoyed by the cry and your focus is on getting the baby to be quiet at that very moment, then you have your own ulterior motive and that's to stop the baby from crying because it's annoying. We're all human; I'm not saying that a baby's cry won't or shouldn't ever annoy you but I'm saying that the moment you become annoyed, your listening skills decrease because you no longer care about the type of cry, you just simply want to stop the cry. So when people come to you for help, maybe about the same thing over and over or maybe it's something simple that you feel is an easy fix, you tend to just think logical and try to make it simple like, for example: "If you think your wife is cheating on you, just divorce her."

Nothing in life is ever just that simple, especially, when time is invested in something or someone. People are very emotional and emotions cause logic to go out the window most of the time, so your advice may be right and it may or may not even end up that way in the future but is a person really ready to hear that? That's what makes listening so hard because as a helper, you start to feel you have all the answers but at the end of the day, you have to handle each situation and individual according to their cry and the only way to do that is to consciously listen and not include yourself while you're helping others.

People also tend to think that what worked for us will also work for others. Now, I can only speak for myself but I know I was not put on this earth to only help people who look like me or think like me; whether it's race, color, cultural background, religion, etc. The challenge and the only way this world will live in peace is if we learn not to only tolerate those different from us but to help and love those who are different from us. I think it's pretty easy to help someone who's exactly like you or have a lot in common because you pretty much agree on everything, for the most part. I love being around people that have the same values, morals, religion, and what not but that's not all life is. My religion is not more right than the next person's; we all serve the same God in different ways, we're on the same team. It's just what works for me and helps make me a better person, what someone else does is their business but that doesn't make us enemies nor should it mean we can't help one another in any way that we can.

I consciously try to challenge myself with every person I meet and come in contact with no matter their race, religion, or beliefs to try to find something that we both enjoy or that we can relate to and enjoy talking about. I've come to realize that talking about your differences is not always a healthy thing, even though it can be. Now, a great healthy debate about your differences is not a bad thing but after so long, you know your religion or whatever you believe in or don't, and it won't change and so do they. With that being said I don't see what's the point of continuing to discuss your differences? The reason we do that is because 1. we feel "God" is on our side in whatever we believe in and 2. we feel it as an obligation to convert people to what we believe in because it's what works for us so we feel it will work for everyone else.

We like to think people are unhappy because they don't have our religion; this is what divides the human race. Like I said earlier in the other chapter, it's not the religion, it's the people. People are flawed, not the religions but that's just my humble opinion. The irony is that when we think this way, we're not really helping someone but we are pushing people away from each other and making them rebellious against religion. What works for you isn't what works for everyone else and maybe, one day, they will be interested in your beliefs but if so, it won't be because of you; that's something that individual has to choose to do personally and that's not something you force on someone. Doing so actually becomes counterproductive. You're not truly helping someone if you're trying to push your own agenda on them.

# THE LORD'S LOVE

L ove is everlasting and God is love. Once we learn to accept God's love and love him first and foremost, then we can possibly love others with imperfections like we have. It's quite difficult to love something or someone that's imperfect before we love The Most High who's perfect. Sometimes, this imperfect world on this short journey called life interferes with our relationship with Christ; there's so many distractions and tools for the devil to use to get us to lose sight of what we need to be focused on. The world is the devil's playground, but we cannot forget that Jesus, himself, conquered the world; that should be all the hope we need when we at times lose focus. We should always have hope and faith in The Lord that he is never done with us no matter how many times we give in to temptation.

It's quite difficult to fathom God's unconditional love when no one in this world could ever come close to loving us how he loves us. If we think our parents, wives, husbands, or family are the ones who love us the most, then we will be constantly disappointed in life. We will often ask the questions, "why am I going through this", "why are bad things always happening to good people", "I did nothing but show love to this or that person and they did me wrong, why me?" We all have been in these situations before and have experienced such frustrations but we're asking the wrong questions.

The question we should be asking ourselves is why are we expecting imperfect human beings to love us like a perfect God loves us? God never promises us that if we treat others well, they will do the same. He encourages us to treat others how we want to be treated and love thy neighbors but we have free will. We have free will to do right or wrong by others. God knows this that's why he put it in scripture, "Never grow weary in doing good things." He said this because he knew the world and people would test us to the point that we question if treating others well is even worth it; that's why he instructs us to do so.

The devil lives for this opportunity when we start to question God. He knows that our human logical mind will at times tune out our spiritual faith in Christ during adversity. We have to remember God never promised us no adversity, he only promised he wouldn't allow us to carry more than we can bear and also that he's always there with us through the adversity. We cannot expect the world and others to love us how God does, this is not only unrealistic but it is a cancer to our relationship with Christ. I read a quote once that said, "For a believer, living in this world is the closest they'll ever be to living in hell and for a non-believer, living in this world is the closest they'll ever be to heaven". This quote is telling believers that we are to bring a little piece of heaven to this world if we allow Christ to use us and live in us and do his work.

I think us believers often times get it twisted and think because we serve God and we're Christians that everything and everyone should treat us right. Living for Christ isn't about being easy, Jesus had it the worse. It's about serving God and accepting the adversity and knowing that the Lord can and will use all things for his good. If there's no test, there's no triumph; if there's no trials and tribulations there can be no testimony. If and when we decide to live for the Lord, then like David said in Psalm 23, we have to be willing to walk "through" the valley of death. If we want to show how big our God is we have to trust in The Lord during our big problems.

One of David's big battles was with Goliath. All odds were against David, just like all odds may be against you right now in life but always remember that's the perfect time for The Lord to show up and show out. If God only allowed problems in our lives that we are confident and comfortable we could handle them on our own, then The Lord would be out of a job. Life will take you to places that are uncomfortable when the only comfort you will have is in God. I'm not saying getting through the adversity is going to be easy, but it's much easier when you have faith that: 1. you're not alone. 2. That eventually it will be okay when it's all said and done. 3. You will be a better and stronger person afterwards.

I always like to say when life is going well, thank God and praise him for the blessing and live in the moment. When things aren't going so well, thank and praise God because it could be worse and also thank him in advance that it won't last forever. This shifts your focus into an attitude of gratitude and that's what we all should be aiming for. Now, you still have to face and deal with the adversity, never run from it, but don't put all of your focus and energy in it because temporary things aren't worth all of you.

For example, if you just started to date and get to know someone, you probably shouldn't (I hope you wouldn't) treat them like they're your husband or wife. Don't put a label on something before you know exactly what it is. That's the way we should view problems in our lives. Just give it a little time before we decide to panic, get angry, or frustrated, and don't give it all of your energy because before we know it, the problem will be gone. In most cases, we'll be able to laugh at it because we usually get all worked up for nothing. We have to get comfortable with being uncomfortable; this is the only way to progress in life.

We must give things, people, situations, and blessings time to reveal what and who they are and know it will always serve a purpose when it's all said and done. Things and people don't always turn out how they seem but that's not always a bad thing. The ugly truth is always better than a pretty dressed up lie. God is our father that knows best, just like our parents when we were growing up would tell us "no" to something we wanted and we never understood why because we just wanted what we wanted. We don't often appreciate our parents until we get older and mature or become parents ourselves. The valuable lesson in this is that God is the same way with us. No matter how old or mature we get with our relationship with God, our father will always know best. This is simple, but as we all know it's not easy to accept when you want what you want.

When I tend to get frustrated with life and God about him not answering my prayers how I think he should, I have to stop and remind myself what I constantly preach to others that God only answers prayers in 3 ways: 1. Yes 2. Not right now. 3. I have something better. This always instantly puts things and life in perspective for me. This reminds me that whatever my heart desires and I pray to The Lord for, I will either get it or God will bless me with something better. That's a win/win, right? I get excited just thinking about it with that mindset because Jesus is so amazing. It's not always easy to trust his timing but it always turns out for the best.

"Trust in The Lord with all of your heart and lean not on your own understanding." I truly believe that our logic and intelligence can and often does interfere with our faith. Quite to the contrary, faith can interfere with logic as well but I don't believe that's often the case. I think more times than not we're too smart for our own good. To make one thing clear, just because you're a person of faith doesn't mean you don't think or use your intelligence. If that was the case, I don't believe God would've given us a brain if he didn't want us to think. My Bishop, Michael Pitts, always says, "I'm always trying to get thinking people to feel something and feeling people to think something and everyone to do something." I love this perspective he uses because he's acknowledging that we all are different and that's not a bad thing but it allows you to know what you need to work on based on your strengths and weaknesses.

I think some people view Christianity from the outside looking in as people who live by these rigid rules and aren't allowed to think, feel, or question anything; this couldn't be further away from the truth. "As a man thinketh so is he" is what it says in the Bible and that's clear as day to let us know the importance of thinking and strongly encourages that you should think the right things. The Lord loves us so much that he did give us free will to do as we may but he knew we would abuse it, that's why he's a forgiving God and loves us unconditionally no matter what we do. There will never be a love more perfect than that.

# DREAMERS

Some people are dreamers, some people aren't, but some people are dreamers that never wake up. A dreamer that never wakes up is just as worse than not being a dreamer. It's a dis-service to yourself, God, and also others that look up to you to have a dream and not wake up to go get it. Dreaming is a start but it's only the beginning. You don't receive anything that you don't pursue. God can open doors but it is us who must take action and step through. Visualizations, dreams, and all of these things are very powerful. They're very powerful because everything starts in the mind, literally. It's also a scientific fact that the mind knows no difference between you visualizing something in your head or you actually physically doing that task. Interesting right?

Sean "Puff Daddy" Combs said it best, "Don't be afraid to close your eyes and dream but then open your eyes and see." This is why you often hear people say everything in life is mental. It's true but it's only part of it. Reality knows the difference between dreaming and waking up. It takes imagination to dream, but it takes courage and action to wake up to pursue it. Waking up takes work, work, and more work. It also involves faith, patience, and prayer. One thing waking up does not include is understanding or in other words, having everything figured out about how to accomplish your dream.

The power of belief is far more powerful than understanding. People who dream and wait to have it all figured out before they wake up often never get pass dreaming; they become spectators to all of those who wake up and take a leap of faith. This is easier said than done because we live in a society today where we want to control and understand everything in life; we like facts and comfort more than faith and being uncomfortable. We don't like to stretch ourselves more than we have to but this is what we need to grow; being uncomfortable. If you didn't know, muscles don't grow unless they're broken down and forced to rebuild themselves up bigger and better to handle the resistance, well our brains and everything else in life is actually no different. We must also accept the fact that breaking down our muscles for them to grow will always be uncomfortable and painful but it's necessary.

We often let our own intellect become our worse enemy. We are so programed to believe that we have go to school, earn a degree, or read a book to become a specialized or a professional in any occupation. There is absolutely nothing wrong with that if that's the route you choose, but one thing that school, books, or formal education cannot teach you is to be a dreamer and follow your heart. In fact, most school systems and teachers are against independent thinking and going against the grain. This is what makes dreaming so hard and scary because most of our lives we are told to think realistically and live safe. This is why a lot of highly successful people were never too fond of school because one, they learn different and two, they're constantly told what to do and what not to do; it doesn't feed positivity to their dreams they have. What they fail to tell us is that thinking and dreaming realistically is what leads to a mediocre lifestyle.

I am an advocate for all and any education because knowledge is power when it's applied properly. I have a Bachelor's Degree from Miami University and it's one of the best things that's ever happened to me. However, I know that college isn't for everyone and I also believe that true education should give you more options, not limit them. I have a degree in Family Studies and I've never used it for that purpose. Literally, all I have used my degree for is to put it down on a resume and use it to be a substitute teacher, which is a blessing in itself.

In fact, I'll admit that my first 3 years after graduating from college and reading hundreds of books on my own, I learned way more useful knowledge on my own versus what I had learned in the classrooms at Miami University. I can't begin to tell you all of the great people and friends and relationships I've built in college that played and still play a huge part in all of my successes today. I built my Master Mind Circle in college as Napoleon Hill likes to call it, which was way more important than getting the degree itself.

*"A friendly alliance with one or more persons who will encourage one to follow through with both plan and purpose"*

*- Napoleon Hill*

Having a degree from Miami University has sparked so many conversations in public settings and even landed me a few jobs off that alone, like I said, it gives you options. I don't think of myself different because I have a degree from one of the top universities in the country but others do and for me to not use that to my advantage,

111

I would be a fool because I worked my butt off to earn that degree. I think we often forget that life has no rules; the only rules that apply to life are the ones you place upon yourself. You have to let go of limited thinking, it will hinder you and people on the outside will feed into that because they, too, have been conditioned to limit themselves. There's more than one way to think as there is also more than one way to live, to be happy, and successful. The only way to live is the way you truly desire to do so and I think it doesn't and shouldn't matter how that is as long as you're happy with what you're doing and not violating the rights of others.

We all have different paths and purposes in life; not everyone will be rich, not everyone will go to college, not everyone will be an entrepreneur, not everyone will be a teacher, firefighter, police officer, actor, doctor, lawyer, or whatever else. You have to find your own way but food for thought; when I go to the doctor and for example and I have to have surgery, I only want a doctor that has the desire to be a doctor. Now, that's an extreme situation but that's my mindset. I only want to be around people that love what they do and I don't care what that may be, just have a passion for it. I mean, wouldn't our education system be better if we had all teachers that actually loved teaching and working with kids? Absolutely, but we all know that's not the case because a lot of people do what they do for the wrong reasons. I think having a passion for what you do is contagious and spreads positive energy to others and helps them seek their true passion. That's success and happiness in a nutshell.

In my circle of friends, I only want people who love what they're doing or pursuing it, period. The only exception is that you're trying to figure out what it is that you love and that doesn't mean sitting around just letting time pass. That takes effort getting to know yourself and finding out what you're passionate about. That involves reading, collaborating with all different kinds of people from different occupations while picking their brains, and studying your own life and past experiences while finding out what's your passion. I think in life, most of the time, I don't know why but it takes for us to experience what we don't want to realize what we do want; this is why temporary failure is not a bad thing, it gets us closer to our dreams. It's not an occupation or money that causes happiness or unhappiness, it's the illusion that we think it's the cause of one or the other from an abundance or lack thereof.

Money is a tool used as a resource that we can never have enough of; it's just like the flesh, it cannot be satisfied. It's like pouring water in a bucket with a hole in it, it's insane to think it will ever work. I've never heard anyone say, "Okay, I have enough money and I don't want any more." There's no amount of money that will make you ever say that; millionaires are the cheapest people on earth, read the book "The Millionaire Next Door". If all you are chasing is money, then you'll never stop running; there is no finish line. On the flip side of the coin, I think some of us think money causes unhappiness or more problems, so to speak. The good book says, "To whom much is given, much is expected." So when you get more, more is expected no matter what it is; it's not just money.

The problem isn't the money itself, it's what we expect the money to bring. Money is a tool that gives you nothing more than options, that's it and it forces you to learn to manage it or your money will eventually leave you. I'm not one to worship money because the good book says the love for money is indeed the root of all evil, not the money itself. I believe with or without money you will have problems; they may be different but you will still have problems and me personally, I would rather have my problems while I have money. If you're financially stable that's one less problem to worry about. We get in trouble with money because for whatever reason we think it solves all problems which is nothing further from the truth. Well, the reason is the media but that's another subject. Money will reveal a lot of things and people's true character, as well as things about yourself, so beware of people who just want your fish instead of trying to learn how to fish for themselves.

I'm not saying don't bless others with your blessings but what I am saying is that "Don't let someone else make their emergencies yours," as Dr. Eric Thomas says. Don't let people drive you to the point to where you feel money caused all of this because it didn't. As I've said, money reveals people and things; it doesn't cause them. Just because something correlates doesn't mean they cause them to happen. A person won't ask you for $1,000 if they don't feel you have it; when they know you have more, they'll ask for more. A person who wouldn't ask you for that money without good reason wouldn't, whether you were broke or rich because that's not who they are. They're not going to ask for it if they don't need it and won't be based on your financial situation, whether you are doing really well or struggling.

The person who would ask based on how well off you are always would, you just never had the money so now that you do, they've revealed themselves by asking for more. I am not making a reference that all people who ask to borrow money are bad people or users, I'm just giving an example of how money can reveal one's true character. When you get money, have a plan for it and make it work for you, don' let it break up friendships or mess up relationships with family; say no before saying yes when you know by giving them money you're not actually helping them. You don't owe a grown person anything and don't let them make you feel like you do. Money is a blessing so use it as such; remember to control it and not let it control you.

A dreamer is someone who dares to see something in them-selves that they haven't yet become. A dreamer isn't afraid to fail, a dreamer isn't afraid to speak and even more importantly, act on their dreams. If you dare to dream, you must be passionate and have enthusiasm because it's hard during the journey and if you don't want it bad enough, you'll eventually quit. If you don't know exactly what you want and have that vision in your head, then you'll end up settling for good instead of great and you'll never get out of your comfort zone. I've learned that most of us are scared to even aim for greatness let alone achieve it. I've learned and observed that greatness and success are very intentional. People who achieve greatness and success set out to do so. People don't receive their blessings and live their dreams because they're scared to even aim for them; it's not that they cannot achieve them.

It's like playing darts and not even attempting to hit the bulls-eye, but we're just content with making it on the board in general where being good is okay. The dangerous thing about being good is if you're surrounded by people who haven't even made it that far, then you "seem" like the success or great one because compared to them, you've made it pretty far and that can cause you to be content and never reach your full potential. Who you associate yourself with is very important to achieve greatness. If you don't aim for the bullseye, you'll never hit it and that's a fact. We do the same thing in life. The bullseye may be harder to hit but it's always worth the extra effort, in fact, your dreams are always worth the time and extra work it'll take.

We're scared to dream because we think pursuing it may not be worth the effort; we know how hard it is so we are scared to even aim that high. If we pay attention and look around, we see this in people every day and I, myself, even had this problem for a long time. When you have something good or when you're already good at something, it takes a special person to not be satisfied with that and to want greatness. As humans, we tend to naturally get comfortable, especially, when we are doing better than the average and most people around us so to others we may be "successful".

I've observed that a lot of people work where they are unhappy, depressed, and hate working where they're currently employed. They constantly complain like they're in jail. You may work a lot of hours and some jobs are harder than others but no one is making you work there; we all have a choice. My question is why don't people leave their jobs if they hate it? People don't leave because they're scared and don't think it's possible that there's anything better. Some people even have other dreams and aspirations but are just scared to pursue them.

Now, I'm not saying just up and quit without a plan, we are all adults and have bills. Maybe come up with a 2, 3, or even a 5 year plan to save money to be able to leave and pursue your real dreams and passions. (It personally took me just a little over two years.) Always remember that there will be some risks and sacrifices; pursing your dreams involves risks and that's the reality of it. People are scared to leave their jobs because after you get your job security, you're at a full-rates pay, and you have all the benefits you literally, never have to worry about getting another job in your life if you choose not to. You can work for 30 years and retire or keep working, either way you're set and most people find comfort in that, which is fine. It's only fine if you're okay with that but if you hate it and you truly want to do something else, then you need to do something about it and START NOW.

We hate to start over once we've worked long and hard to get to a certain point at our job, or in life in general, we feel entitled to relax and get comfortable. Starting over and taking a risk scares the crap out of all of us, I don't care who you are. The difference in the dreamers is that it's not that they don't have fears but they just simply face them. They see the possible in the impossible, their passion and drive for their dreams outweigh their fears and comfort zone. The great news about fear and faith is that they both weigh however much you want them to weigh. If you want a lot of faith, then feed your faith; if you want a lot of fear, then keep feeding your doubts and accepting it. The reason it's so hard to feed faith, like I stated earlier, is that it involves risk; the risk to fail and it not work out how you had it planned.

I'm not the smartest man in the world but I do know one thing for sure and that is that there are only two ways that will guarantee that you will fail. 1. To not try. 2. To quit. If you try with everything you have, you cannot fail. If you never quit, you cannot fail. (Read that last sentence again aloud.) Me, personally, I've learned to embrace "failures" because it simply means I'm closer to success. When I have "temporary failures" (what I like to call failures), I now know something I didn't before; you must keep going. It has been recorded that Thomas Edison failed 10,000 times before he successfully invented the light bulb; I'm so glad he didn't give up. Big credit goes to Lewis Latimer who helped Thomas Edison get over that last hump with the light bulb.

Failures and setbacks are stepping stones to success. It's harder to go up than it is to go down. Steps on a staircase represent failures you have to step on and over to move up closer to the top. Most of us quit in the middle of going up the steps. Everyone starts out hard and enthusiastic headed toward their dreams. However, just like climbing steps, the closer you get to the top, the harder it gets because you've been climbing for so long already; this lets you know the harder it gets, the closer you are to the top, remember that.

Another reason we quit is because after climbing halfway up the steps, you may be considered "good" and people may even tell you that you're successful, but we cannot settle for being good or being the exception. We must know deep down inside that we have a lot more room to grow and improve. Your expectation of yourself can and should be nothing less than greatness. Just because you've made it further than someone else and you seem successful to them doesn't mean you stop climbing because you know there's still more steps left. That's where it goes back to aiming for your dreams and goals and making them "unrealistic"; you can't expect people to understand your hunger.

I have a friend and he and I both were signed up to take the Toledo Firefighter Civil Service Examination. So in the 30 days or so we had to study, we would occasionally ask each other how studying was going. I vividly remember a conversation we had where I asked him how studying was going he said, "It's going really good. I'm going to get in the top 20." (Top 20 is a great score and would give him a good chance to get into the fire academy.) I texted him back and said, "Why not go to be in the top 3?" He said, "That's doing too much, top 20 is good for me." If I remember correctly, I think I just texted him back "laughing out loud" at his comment and left it at that because I didn't want his top 20 mindset to wear off on me.

As I mentioned earlier I wrote down that I was going to score #1 on this test and that was my goal. I read and prayed over that every single day for about a year. Did I score #1? No, I did not, I ranked #90 out of 920 other people who passed the test. What do you think my friend scored? He didn't rank in the 920 at all. Was it that I'm smarter than him? Not at all. I truly believe he's more book smart than I am. Did I study more than him? Maybe, who knows, I just know I studied as hard as I possibly could with the time I had available to score number one. I believe more than anything else our mindsets and expectations we had for ourselves is what separated us.

I wasn't scared to attempt to be #1 and not get it where he was willing to settle for top 20 and I wasn't. Why do people set the bar low? I truly believe whether we're conscious of it or not, it's because we can say I really didn't want it or I didn't try my best if it doesn't work out how we planned for it. We're scared to fail to reach what we set out to do. I wanted to be great and the best but he was okay with just getting by. When you set your goals and dreams high and aim high, you will put more effort in; it's harder to give up or settle. It was like he just wanted to make the playoffs but I wanted to win the championship. IT'S A MINDSET and it has nothing to do with talent or ability.

It's not about talent or intelligence those are things you have limited control over. But you control your mindset, the size of your dreams, and how high you set the bar. I set the bar at #1, which is the highest and I scored pretty high even though I didn't get #1 but that's not the point because that was my goal and I believed I could do it. He set the bar lower than me and that's exactly the results he got; he wanted to be farther from number 1 than me (his words not mine) and that's what happened, our goals were accurate according to what we both dared to ask for.

Set your bar high is all I'm trying to tell you. It will stretch you to do more to reach it because you know it will take more out of you to reach your own expectations. The power of expectations and exceptions are such a huge influence in our lives, whether we realize it or not. All dreamers have one goal in mind and that is to make their dreams a reality. It can be scary and discouraging when all you have is your dream because there's no proof for your vision; the one thing of yours that you can see clearly that others can't.

# SETTING THE BAR

The bar you set will remain the bar you reach for until you raise the bar again. No one sets out to be just good and somehow accidentally achieves greatness. No one aims to finish 3rd place and finishes first; success, greatness, happiness, and becoming the best you that you can possibly be is never on accident, it's always intentional. The best comparison for what I'm trying to describe is the high jump event in track in field. The rules are pretty simple, set the bar at the height that you choose and jump over it without knocking down the bar. What's unique about this event is that you and only you decide the height that the bar is set at, this is no different than setting the bar for your dreams and goals in life.

The choice always was and always will be yours. In the high jump, once you set the bar, it stays at that specific height until you clear it then you keep raising it higher and higher from there; you can only go up. In the high jump, you get 3 attempts to clear each height you set the bar at, but in life, every day you wake up is an opportunity to jump again. What's interesting about setting the bar at the height you choose is that if you set it at 6 feet and you clear it successfully with 6 more inches to spare, you do not get credit for

6 feet and 6 inches because you only get credit for clearing the 6 feet you set it at. Why is this so important? It's important because however high or low you decide to set the bar is how high or low you'll attempt to jump; you'll never jump higher if you don't have the courage to set the bar higher. This is life, one does not achieve more than they dare to set out to do; to desire more and be hungry for more is the first step to accomplishing and becoming more.

Wherever you set the bar is exactly what you're going to reach for, no matter how high or low, if you thought you could do more, you would simply set the bar higher; if we knew better we would do better but it all starts with believing. The key thing and probably the most important thing we must remember when setting the bar is that our mind often talks us out of things that our body can actually do. Your body can do just about anything that your mind gives it direction to do. With faith, hard work, dedication, and persistence, the only limits you have are the ones you believe and place on yourself. We tend to sell ourselves short instead of reaching to set the bar higher than what we think we can achieve. The world shrinks or expands to the capacity of our thinking.

If someone grows up in a small town, of say 1,000 people, in Ohio and they never leave that small town their entire life then that's the only world they'll ever know as they see it. It's not them physically leaving that city that's so important compared to them expanding their minds just knowing there's more even when they can't see it. Knowing that there's more out there to explore and knowing the endless possibilities make you a contender when on the road to become healthy, happy, and successful. We must first have the guts to set the bar high before we even worry about how we're going to jump over it, that is always the first step even though we tend to think the process is the other way around; we must first dare to be great.

Most people don't know what more is because they've never been around it, let alone experienced it. They may see people on TV or read about people living abundantly and happy but they don't believe they can become whatever they put their minds to doing. On the other end, some people do know but they just don't feel worthy and they just continue to live a life setting the bar low and being average. When you are bold enough to set the bar higher, that alone in itself will lead you to new opportunities and you will surprise yourself to what you can actually do compared to what you thought you could do. Getting out of our comfort zone is the key to success. If you don't look up at that bar from time to time and wonder how the hell you're going to jump over it, then you haven't set the bar high enough yet.

I say this to my friends and family all the time; your dreams and goals should scare the crap out of you because this way it demands more out of you than we, at times, demand of ourselves. Once we set ourselves up and constantly challenge our comfort zone, it's very important that we stick to it; just like in the high jump, once you pick a height you can never lower the bar, NEVER LOWER THE BAR. You may not always get the exact results you're looking for and that's okay but in the midst of reaching for that high bar, you'll learn more great things about yourself that you have inside which is better than winning or clearing the bar could ever teach you. This should go without saying but, you shouldn't be playing anything if you're not playing to win.

The mentality to win and compete is far more important than the winning result itself. When you set the bar high winning just becomes a by-product of your ultimate goal. For an example, if a high school football team sets out to win a state-championship then winning is a by-product; they have to win a lot more than they lose to be able to get there. Winning a state championship will include winning a city title, district title, and regional championship as well, so these things don't need to be discussed because it comes along with the high bar goal of winning the state title.

My point is that if you work hard and give 100%, winning will happen regardless over time so that shouldn't be your main focus and where you seek value from. The goal is to continue to get better, keep setting the bar higher and higher beyond your comfort zone. People who win and get comfortable are the people who get a taste of success and never taste it again and wonder why. The reason why is because they forgot what it took to get there; they think success somehow carries over or that it gets easier but I'm here to tell you personally that's a lie.

Nothing in life gets easier, especially, success and nothing is harder than to continue to repeat your success because different levels of success have different devils. There's always a new challenge waiting for you each time you set the bar higher to achieve more. Every height requires a different ingredient to be successful. We tend to become frustrated when our old ways don't work for our new challenges. It's simple, use what works and change what doesn't and keep it moving from there. The average person should think you're crazy for how high you set the bar for yourself.

We must remember that we must not shrink our dreams and all that we want to become because it may offend or not make sense to others. The world is limitless and God gave us the power to become whatever it is that we want to be but God also says ask and you shall receive. It takes faith to ask because people don't ask if they don't believe they can possibly get it. Set that bar higher than you think you can jump and if you can't jump that height but you do everything in your power to do it, God will show up at the perfect time and give you wings to achieve your dreams.

# EXPECTATIONS VERSUS EXCEPTIONS

**Exception:** -noun 1. something excepted; an instance or case not conforming to the general rule.

**Expectation:** -noun 1. the act or the state of expecting to wait in expectation 2. the act or state of looking forward or anticipating 3. an expectant mental attitude a high pitch of expectation.

E xpectations and exception start from the day we are born until the day we grow to adults and it continues until the day we leave this earth. Very similar in spelling with a very similar root word but these two terms have two totally different meanings and will have the opposite impact on an individual depending on which one and how it's pitched to the individual. This chapter "Expectations versus Exceptions" is nothing more than my thoughts comparing the two.

I will kind of play devil's advocate in some instances against myself on my view on the two but I will give you good reasons because I think both can be used either way; so this may seem quite complex but just work with me as I'll try my best to explain why. When I got the idea to write this chapter it was from a friend named, Morris Council, who at the time was in school to receive his Doctorate Degree. Morris and I played football together at Miami University; a great friend of mine and a great individual. He sparked the idea for me to write this chapter and I thank him for that sincerely.

As I said, expectations and exceptions start from the day we are born and continue for the rest of our lives. At some point in our lives, the expectations from our parents or whoever raised us and what they considered exceptions are all that really matters coming from them. Our parents are, for lack of better terms, God like figures and what they say and think of you means more than anything in the world to us. At some point, in my opinion, when we are usually teenagers, we start to feel a sense of independence and form our own expectations and what we consider the exceptions for ourselves; in other words, we realize what we think of ourselves really matters, not just what our parents think and expect. At another point, we will start to date and have a girlfriend or boyfriend and their opinions will mean the world to us, too.

This can last past our teen years up into about our 20's and this can possibly cause a problem because a very vindictive person can use this against us to sabotage our relationship with our parents. It sounds absurd but anyone who has ever had a strong liking for someone or ever been in love knows that love can be very blinding and you do some crazy things when you "think" you're in love. I say "think" because if someone really loves you, they don't try to sabotage any other relationships in your life, especially, the ones with your parents. For better or for worse, you have to stay in your place and let that person figure things out if their parents control their lives through their expectations of them.

After that stage of expectations and exceptions with your significant, other you will eventually reach a mature adult stage when it comes to expectations and exceptions. You will then realize that everyone in your life will have expectations of you and what they consider to be the exception of things but you will also realize that the most important ones are the ones you have for yourself. Not that friends and family member's opinions don't matter but if it's not what you want or want to become, then what they think is irrelevant and if they respect you enough they can do nothing but respect your decisions.

It can also work the other way around. A friend or family member's expectations of you can build and keep your confidence up to go after what you really do want out of life. As we all know, if you live life long enough, at times it can and will be discouraging and we all need someone sometimes because life is hard regardless; there is no easy way out so you might as well go after what you really want, dream, and live big.

If you vent to a friend, it can be very critical if they play the exception or expectation card when they give you advice. For an example, if you enroll in college after high school and after the first semester on winter break you are debating on dropping out because you decide college is not for you; maybe it's too difficult and you don't really need college to be successful. Now, I'm not saying that it's not true that you don't "need" college to be successful or anything of that nature, college is for anybody who wants to go. College or education in general (not just school) could and has never hurt anyone, it will only help you because it simply gives you more options if you take advantage of it like you should. It maybe can hurt you financially but to me education, life lessons, relationships, and developing and learning who you are and what you want to become are priceless things and that is what college does for you. It's way more than just the degree; that's just a byproduct.

At the end of the day, we all know you need to first spend money to make money. Going back to the example, we'll say the individual always wanted to attend college and graduate and they're the first one in their family to even attend college so when that person is saying that you don't need college to be successful, they're saying that out of frustration. They're using it as a way to justify if they decide to not go back to school because deep down inside the person knows that college is what they really want. (This is not always the case but just an example.)

When this is talked about to a friend with high expectations of the friend who's thinking about dropping out, they will be very blunt and explain how it won't be easy but it's not impossible to get through college. They will explain that they should want better opportunities than what that person's family had and college will only increase those chances. They will remind that friend that all they talked about was graduating college since they were kids and that it was always their dream and that they should never expect less or settle for anything less than that.

A friend with good expectations will tell that friend who's going through that tough time that there is no other option but to graduate because they've come too far and this is what will happen; you will finish. It's no different than a coach having high expectations for his or her players, a coach's job is to have higher expectations than the player has for themselves and to get more out of the player than they ever thought they could get out of themselves. This ends up being a life lesson, not just a sport lesson; we can always do more than we think we can. This sometimes requires tough love but they will always thank you later for it; we need friends, family, mentors, coaches, and significant others like this, people who believe in us when we don't believe in ourselves, the ones that have high expectations for us.

A friend with more of the exception attitude will not pull the best out of that friend who's debating on not going back to school next semester. An exception attitude will let that friend have the pity party and probably agree with everything they're saying like how it's hard and college may not be for them and so on; pretty much all excuses. The exception friend cannot distinguish that college being hard and college not being for someone are two totally different things. College is for that friend if that's always been their dream since they were young; they arrived at a hurdle in life they have to overcome. They just didn't think college would be this challenging and now they simply don't want to face it. There will be adversity on every journey we decide to take on the way to our goals is what we at times fail to realize. A friend of exception won't tell that friend that all things worth having are worth fighting for and what you really want you should never quit going after. This friend doesn't understand that if they allow their friend to quit now, they'll be quitting for the rest of their lives while pursuing things they really want.

It's not that you can't be sensitive and empathize with what they're going through but at the end of the day, you have to build that person back up and remind them of the expectations they have of themselves. It won't be easy because they are in the midst of the storm but hey, that's why good friends are hard to come by because they will do whatever it takes to get you to believe in yourself again; that's what good friends do no matter what. A friend with an exception attitude may say things like, "Well at least you attended college unlike any of your family members and you just discovered it wasn't for you and you should be proud of that." I am not saying this is wrong but this is where you have to really know your friends because if all they talked about growing up was graduating from college, then you know that desire does not just disappear after one difficult semester.

We all need that little push from time to time and, like I said earlier, it's just tough love but it's so necessary because life is hard and quitting is easy, but living with the regret that you quit on something you really still wanted may be the hardest thing ever in life. College is just one example; this can be applied to anything. We must also be aware that this type of friend isn't jealous or envious of us; some of our "friends" don't mind seeing us do well as long as it's not better than them. We must identify these people in our lives and stay away from them.

I was raised in a single parent household by my mother and my earliest memory of her having high expectations for me was when it came to my grades. I don't remember exactly how old I was but it was probably around when I was in the 8th grade maybe, so about 13-14 years old, give or take. I remember talking to my peers and a lot of them would say that when they got A's on their report cards, their parents would give them money for each A. I vividly remember thinking, "Well I get just about straight A's on my report card so that's a great idea and a way I could make some easy money." I remember coming to my mom with this proposal and her instantly shutting down the idea by saying, "Little boy, you're supposed to get good grades, you don't get rewarded for things you're supposed to do." That was the end of that discussion, but little did I know, that would be a life lesson that would stick with me for the remainder of my childhood and continue to becoming an adult.

My mom expected me to earn good grades and demanded I did so because that is what I should do; it's the right thing to do, try my best to be the best. If I had an easy A versus a hardworking C grade, then the A really doesn't mean anything. My mom always taught me to do my best and fortunately my best effort was good enough to get just about straight A's and B's throughout high school. Do my best at everything is one of the best lessons my mother taught me. Don't get me wrong, my mom always congratulated me and made sure she acknowledged my "effort" that it took to get those grades, which is more important than the grade itself but there's a difference and a fine line between that and her praising me as if getting good grades and trying my best was an exception to the rule.

If she thought that was the exception and constantly rewarded me when I did what I was "supposed" to do, then my motivation would have been a lot different as a kid and an adult. If my mom thought getting good grades was an exception as a kid then as I became an adult, I would've thought handling my responsibilities that comes with being an adult deserves some kind of praise, which sounds a crazy if you ask me but people are this way all the time and I see it every day.

It's pretty much over all social networks, people claiming that they're "independent" saying they have their own house, car, take care of their kids, etc. Well, I thought those are things you're supposed to do as an adult, right? You should not expect a pat on the back for doing something that you're supposed to do. I mean, if you bring a kid into this world that's your choice, not the kid's so they're your responsibility and you don't get an applause for that because that's part of being a parent. To have a job, house, and a car I mean, shouldn't all adults have those things? If they don't, they should at least be striving for them.

I think the correlation from parents having expectations to when we become adults will play a major role in your mindset as an adult. Parents will have high expectations for their children and demand nothing but their best and when they do good, they acknowledge their good effort and behavior. They also let them know that's what they should be doing anyway and should never expect a reward for that, even though sometimes they may get something for it but don't expect it. When parents praise and constantly give rewards for behavior and actions because they believe it's the exception, then that will program that child to think they should get something for doing what they're supposed to do. This may be harmless as a kid because this may motivate the kid to get great grades and they may actually do so but when they become adults, this mindset will remain the same. They will think the world owes them something as an adult because they're handling their responsibilities just like the next person. This will hinder that person because they will always feel like the world is unfair and when they do something, they're always expecting something in return.

What someone expects from you can say a lot about the role that that person plays in your life. That lets them know how they view you and the potential they see in you, or lack thereof. One thing that's even more important is the expectations of yourself. For me personally, I take a lot of pride in never letting my expectations of myself be lower than someone else's expectations of myself. I just will not allow this to happen because when someone else's expectations of yourself are higher than yours, then you start to feel a form of pressure that you have to live up to and I refuse to live my life based on someone else's expectations. I'm not saying that someone having good and high expectations of you is a bad thing, all I'm saying is that you should expect more of yourself than what others expect of you because you're the one that has to live with you.

It's very important to keep people around you with high expectations of you because these people are important, like I said earlier, when times get rough and you start to doubt yourself. It's very helpful and healthy to have these kinds of people in your corner and in your support system. Everyone we keep in our circle needs to be checked, we need to know what they bring to our lives; are they adding or taking away. If they're adding, then they should remain in our circle and we should be adding to their lives as well, it's not a one way street; we are all about the win/win opportunities. If someone is in our circle and all we're doing is adding to their lives and they're taking away from ours, then these are not people with high expectations for us; they need to be cut off and kicked out of our circle.

# AIRPLANE

Driving 75 mph on Interstate 75 North headed to Detroit, Michigan, it's only about a 45-minute drive and it seems like less if you're having great conversation. I had just got done working a 10-hour shift, standing on my feet building Jeeps in a factory all day. Driving there wasn't my biggest concern, it was the rules and the process I was going to have to abide by when I reached my destination in Detroit. We all have a choice to follow rules or laws but in this case, for my situation, if I wanted to get to where I was going then the rules were non-negotiable. I've been in this situation so many times that I've mastered dressing comfortable; sweat pants, comfortable tennis shoes, and anything that can be checked or taken off to be checked as quickly as possible to save time. No food or drinks which may be my biggest pet peeve of all the rules because I love my snacks but they have snacks you can buy once you're cleared, of course the prices are jacked sky high. You may not like these rules but you will follow them, you may not like the process to greatness and success but if you don't follow the rules, you'll never fly like you were born to do.

If anyone has ever flown on an airplane in general, not even going to another country but just to go anywhere everyone knows, the least exciting part about flying is going through security checks, getting your bags checked, boarding passes, and all that fun stuff. It's even to another extreme leaving and coming from out the country going through customs, as I found out. This entire process is so thorough that it can drive the most patient person to feel like they have no patience at all. We all know they make you check your bag, weigh your bag, take off your shoes, empty your pockets, hand search you, and at one point they even checked and went through my hair (I had long dreadlocks at the time), which I felt was a bit absurd but it was part of the process. When you're trying to get somewhere, everything in between that just seems to be in the way so we think it just makes the entire process that much more annoying for us. Ironically, on my way to Dominican Republic, it didn't seem as bad I guess because I was just excited for the trip and all the waiting just seemed like minor hurdles to get to my final destination; plus, I was all for just enjoying the process.

Now, quite to the contrary, on the way back from Dominican was just somewhat frustrating and tested my patience to the max. On the way back, I traveled a total of 12 hours and only about 5 hours of it was flying time and the other 7 was in airports going through customs and all the procedures to get back into the U.S. I was exhausted from the vacation, I was feeling under the weather, and I also knew I still had to drive an hour back home when I finally landed in Detroit, MI; my home is in Toledo, OH. So as you can see, it was just a pretty stressful and lengthy trip on the way back that I kind of let get the best of me and my patience. At the same time, I am very big on positive thinking and at the time I was not practicing what I preached.

I must admit that God works in mysterious ways and while I was waiting in that airport trying to get back home, he began to talk to me and make a positive thing out of my situation. The message came in a flash to me and the message was, "Why don't we check the people and things prior to when we let them in our lives how the airport checks us and our luggage before we get on their airplanes?" When this message popped in my head, all I could say was "WOW" what a great question, then I began to brainstorm and elaborate mentally on the question and it all started to make sense; how great of an analogy it was.

If we want to fly and achieve greatness how God planned in our lives, then we cannot bring and keep unnecessary luggage and people in our lives that will weigh us down and hinder us from flying to new heights. When you fly, you cannot bring everything and everyone with you. We are our own greatest investment and I think at times we often forget that. I'm also a firm believer that life is about helping others but we also have to keep in mind that we cannot help others if we have not first helped ourselves and we cannot truly help others until they first help themselves as well. You are the airline, it's your brand, if you want a lot of others to fly, you have to first get your plane off the ground.

I'm all for avoiding problems before they arise or learning from other's mistakes but at the end of the day, we are human and we may let someone or something in our lives that may be toxic to us; that's when it's time to do an airport security check on our own lives every once in a while, and filter those things and people out so we can achieve greatness. Just like at the airport, they tell you the bag can't be over this weight or you can't bring liquids into the airport but people still bring oversized bags and liquids all the time. The airport security doesn't get upset, they just simply take your liquids and tell you to throw them away or have you take things out of your luggage to reduce the weight; they don't care at all how you feel about it, believe me, I found out from experience, there's no exceptions to the rules.

This is how we need to treat our own lives with things and people we don't need that aren't going to help us fly and achieve greatness. When you're trying to be great and live for God's purpose for your life, we have to draw a bottom line and people need to qualify to be in our lives; this is not being selfish, this is self-love. Your life is all you have and all you have is one so it's not about trying to please everyone and trying not to offend everyone because at times, you just have to cut people and things off to get closer to God to reach your full-potential.

I remember vividly one time I had just got cut from the Nebraska Danger Indoor professional football team and I was flying back home from Nebraska, pretty much frustrated for them letting me go off the team and one of my bags was overweight. I think the lady could feel my energy that I wasn't in the best of moods and she was a very nice lady but when my bag was overweight none of that mattered, she just simply said in a nice way, "You have to take some stuff out young man." I didn't give her any attitude about it but I can't say I didn't feel a certain type of way about it just because of what I was going through at the time. This is a perfect example for our lives because we cannot worry about offending people or worry about what they will think of us if we're trying to be all we were born to be.

Just think how perfect everything has to be when they build an airplane; the shape, the maintenance, GPS, the pilot, flight stewardess and their checklist, the weight of the luggage has its limits, and the list goes on. The passengers even play a major role, if there are no passengers then fuel for the airplane can't be paid for, the pilots can't be paid, the flight stewards, etc. So the people on the plane and in your life are very important, but who, as in quality of the people is most important. You're not going to let a person book a flight that has an expired credit card that isn't going through when they book their flight and just say, "Oh, you can pay later." No, that's not how it works but we often let people in our lives like this, people who we are always giving and giving more to the point it doesn't help them or you. We need to check people how the airport does in our lives to that extreme if we want to achieve greatness.

The quality of people is important but so is the quantity also. If the plane has only 200 seats for passengers then they're not going to book 205 people because there is simply no room for them; you can't give them a seat so you're not going to take their time or money. This translates to our lives to where we can't help everyone; we're limited individuals, we're not God, we can't do everything, only He can so we should never feel bad for being humble and not biting off more than we can chew. It's nothing wrong with telling people, "Sorry but all the tickets on this flight are sold out, maybe you can catch the next flight." An airline doesn't change its itinerary for one person and we shouldn't' change our lives for one person who may miss you when they had the chance. Maybe next time around you'll be able to help them and they'll be able to help you but right now your life is booked with these people, these priorities, dreams, and goals and you just don't have the extra time to provide.

When you're running or going forward, you cannot look back; it's a scientific fact that when you look back, you slow down and that's why your head is forward when you run. This is why in track and field sprint relay races they do a blind hand-off exchange with the baton, because if you look back it will slow you down so they practice countless hours of handing off the baton without looking and keeping their head forward; those milliseconds can make the difference between winning and losing.

The things, people, and situations we have to let go to take flight in our lives needs to be exactly that; let go. I firmly believe God allows things and people in our lives for certain seasons for different reasons but the real test is when we want to become better and spread our wings to fly. Will we be able to let those things go so He can give us the new blessings He has waiting for us as soon as we make room for them. The question simply comes down to how do you treat your own private plane, which is you? Do you make room for the people and the luggage that doesn't belong, that needs to be left behind based on your bottom lines you've made in your life? Or do you make room for God to allow you to fly and achieve greatness and for you to have the best flight possible?

When you want to be great, it comes with a lot of responsibility and discipline, just like how the airport does when they put us through their procedures. Discipline, I think, is most important when it comes to this because we often let our feelings interfere with discipline with everything in our lives. The decisions and commitments we make has to outweigh our temporary feelings we have some days; the airline doesn't care if the workers don't feel like thoroughly checking someone's luggage, they simply have to do it. In our lives it can't matter if we feel like going to the gym, feel like cutting off a relationship, friendship that's poisonous, practicing our craft, leaving that job and taking a leap of faith; feelings often interfere with faith. We get so attached to things and people that we really believe we can't go without them, when to the contrary, we can go further and achieve greater things and fly without them. We love our comfort zones but the only way to grow and get better is to get comfortable with being uncomfortable. Feelings often times get in the way of greatness but that's where discipline and bottom lines come in. The great Dr. Eric Thomas said, "At the end of your feelings there's nothing, but at the end of every principle is a promise." I couldn't agree more with this quote.

By no means am I saying not to help people who cannot help you; I am a firm believer that we must help people the most who cannot do anything for us in return. It's not about taking from people but it's about if you're helping someone and it's bringing you down, then you're not really helping them because, eventually, you will get fed up and resent that person. Even if you continue to help them, it will be out of guilt and that's not good either. Sometimes it's hard to accept the fact that with certain people when you help them, it's really not helping them. We often overestimate our abilities to help others in life but we fail to realize that the only people that can truly be helped are the people that want to first help themselves; that's where it always has to start.

No matter how influential you think you are or how good you are at motivating people, it has to start with them. So giving people a free flight or money, time, and chance after chance is really not doing them any service. For example, if you keep giving someone money to get their life together and all they keep doing is going to buy drugs with that money and you know this then you are not helping them. At that point, you're just doing it either out of guilt or just to make yourself feel better. Helping people can never be about you.

So how do you treat your private plane, which is you? Do you keep up with the maintenance? Do you let just anybody fly on your airplane? Do you let them not go through a security check before they get on your plane because they're so called "friends and family"? We must learn to respect our lives how the airport and airlines respect their airplanes. Everything and everyone on that airplane is accounted for, all the passengers have paid their dues in some way, shape, or form to get on that airplane; otherwise, they wouldn't be there. I think we can learn a lot from airports about who we allow in our lives and who we allow to take flight when we decide to spread our wings and be great.

We have to let go of the illusion that we can take everyone with us, everyone is not ready to fly; they'll only hinder you and what you're trying to do. You cannot expect them to understand your vision because if they're not ready, there's nothing you can do about it. As annoying as it is going through airport security and checking my bags before getting on an airplane, I thank God that they do it because I'm sure there would be a lot worse things happening with terrorist attacks if they didn't stick with their security procedures. My advice if you want to fly and be great is to get all the extra luggage and people out of your life that's serving no purpose and don't even have a ticket to get on the plane. These people just want the "hook up" but beware of these people because successful people don't expect favors, they work for what they want and they would not have it any other way.

# WHAT'S THE WORST THAT CAN HAPPEN?

*"How do you grow? Get uncomfortable real quick and you'll start growing. You have to be comfortable with being uncomfortable"*

*- Anonymous*

What's the worst that could happen if you put all of your eggs in one basket? We hear people say "don't put all of your eggs in one basket" so much it gets planted in our subconscious mind without us even questioning the question and asking why not? I thought it would be an interesting topic to discuss that's very relevant to our everyday lives. I'm sure we've all been told by someone or said to others "never put all of your eggs in one basket." I can somewhat understand why someone would say that but I cannot say that I agree with it 100%. When it comes down to it, I believe that not putting all of your eggs in one basket is a safe way to live and a popular thing to do. I'm not sure why but I've never been too fond of the one foot in and one foot out strategy when it came to anything in life because if anything matters then everything does. I'm talking things such as commitment to your dreams, sports, school work, goals, relationships, and whatever else you can name. How can one fully receive the benefit of something or someone if you're not 100% invested? With that being said, I do believe there's a time and place for everything.

The first step is always figuring out what you want and how bad do you really want it. This is a decision that one has to make in life about a lot of things; religion, love, education, money, relationships, careers, the list is infinite. I think it's safe to say that the more eggs you crack open and scramble in a skillet, the more scrambled eggs you'll have on your plate when they're done. Is this not true also in our lives? We have to pay for what we get; the more eggs in the basket, the heavier it'll be and the more your arm may hurt carrying that basket. You may have to set the basket down and rest, you may need someone to help you carry the basket at times or motivate you to keep carrying it, people will laugh at you, call you crazy but you'll be better for it and in the end, you'll have more blessings than the one who feared putting all of their eggs in one basket.

Before I continue, I want to make it clear that I am not saying that you shouldn't have options; options are always good and necessary according to each individual and their situation. I know one thing, we only get one life and I think we all have a purpose and it's hard to live your purpose and be phenomenal at it when you are scared of fully committing to that purpose. If we are scared to carry a heavy basket with all of our eggs then we are probably also scared of bigger blessings that the Lord has planned for us. "For unto whomsoever much is given, of him shall be much required:

and to whom men have committed much, of him they will ask the more." [Luke 12:48] This verse describes what I am trying to explain perfectly. If you commit more, you'll get more. If you invest more, your return will be much greater; it's quite simple.

We cannot fear dropping the eggs, we cannot fear what other's opinions are about what we do with our eggs, you cannot expect for someone who's full off two scrambled eggs to understand when you have a dozen eggs in your basket and you're planning to make an omelet! All you need to know in your mind is that it's possible and that you will do it. They will not understand you and you shouldn't waste your time trying to convince them to do so. One major and important difference we must remember is the time it takes to make two scrambled eggs versus the time it takes to make an omelet. They'll be eating their two scrambled eggs in say, 3 minutes but your omelet will take much longer to cook. They'll be eating and saying to you, "I told you to just make scrambled eggs, it doesn't take as long and I didn't have to buy as many eggs." First off, don't listen to this person who is okay with being average and second, if this isn't a person who you have to communicate with as in a family member or co-worker, you should cut them off completely; they're not helping you with all of your eggs in your basket because they have a different mindset. If it's someone you must deal with on a regular basis, then just don't discuss your eggs and your basket with them because they'll discourage you.

They have a scrambled egg mindset but you know that you not only want more than scrambled eggs, you know that God created you for more. If that person is scared to carry a basket with more eggs then that's fine, don't try to convince them to think like you because they'll see soon enough. You're not any better than them, you're just different and your appetites differ and that's okay. These are the type of people that are content with a job because it pays good and has benefits, even though they literally hate going to work every day. God gives us what our heart desires and how much we invest in that makes it possible. They'll be eating their scrambled eggs and when your omelet gets done, their eyes will get big and say one of two things: "Aw man, I should've taken the extra time and used more eggs and made one, too" or "Can I have some of your omelet?" I don't know about you but I don't share my food. (That was a joke, not a correct correlation to blessings which I am talking.)

Always share your blessings because this is the way to show people that The Lord has been great to you by committing to him, your purpose and blessings are meant to be shared because you never know what that can do for someone. That reaction is exactly how they will react and it's meant for people like you to inspire people like that. It's nothing but a mindset, but the mindset to put more eggs in the basket requires faith, hard work, great people, perseverance, prayer, and Christ, himself, most importantly. If you look at a lot of successful people and how they spend their time and distribute their eggs, it's evident that they put most, if not all, of their eggs in one basket. The more they carried, the bigger their blessings were even though in the midst of them carrying the basket, it looked as if they were going nowhere; they were just preparing one gigantic omelet, little did everyone know.

The even more interesting thing to me while studying successful people who put a lot of eggs in one basket is that after they get that omelet, they start to get an appetite for other big meals like steak, baked potatoes, and things of that sort. This is where the egg distribution tends to start; it opens up so many more blessings because one wasn't scared to carry that heavy basket. Once you learn how to carry one heavy basket, it becomes a piece of cake to carry a whole bunch of light baskets. You can study any successful person and I promise you'll see one thing in common, they became phenomenal at one thing by putting in a lot of time on it; they mastered it and it opened up many all other types of opportunities.

You can look at someone like entrepreneur, business man, and rapper, Sean Carter better, known Jay-Z. He started as a poor kid from Marcy Projects in Brooklyn, NY committed to rapping (put all his eggs in), gave up drug dealing, became a great rapper, opened up new opportunities, started his own clothing line, invested in a NBA team, and started a sports agency. Steve Harvey went to college, quit school, committed to becoming a comedian (all eggs in), became a comedian, new opportunities, own TV show, and author. Arnold Schwarzenegger committed to becoming a body builder, became the best, new opportunities, actor, author, and politician. I can go on and on with an infinite list of successful people that put all of their eggs in one basket and became great which opened up more doors than one.

I don't believe these things happened by coincidence, they all paid their dues by carrying heavy baskets and none of their journeys with those baskets were easy. They wanted the omelet more than they were worried about carrying a heavy basket or someone in their ear being negative. You have to want what you want more than the fear of not getting it. I think that's the main reason people are scared to carry a basket with all of their eggs because of what might not happen and honestly, that's understandable from a logical standpoint; however, life requires faith and my faith is in my Lord Jesus Christ. I say that to say since I've accepted him, it became evident how much I don't know and don't have figured out about life and it taught me life is not so much about logic and always understanding things. I know that the things I want in life, I cannot be scared to go after them. I know if I want bigger blessings,

I have to carry a basket with more eggs, there's no way around that but what I don't know and what I don't have figured out is really not my problem or focus. I do know I will get through it because I can do all things through Christ who strengthens me. [Phil 4:13]

God puts inside you your heart's desires and your purpose, it's our job to figure out what that is then it's our job to go after that with all the eggs we have and trust that the Lord will make it work before we know how he will do so; that's faith and that's life. God is love and He'll never fail you. I didn't write this to tell you where to put your eggs or that you need to put them all in one basket but I wrote it to tell you and encourage you to ask yourself where do YOU really want all of your eggs? Be honest with yourself and put them there and enjoy your omelet because it's the only thing that will be fulfilling for your life's hunger.

You'll only get better at something by failing at it. This may sound weird but it's true, the people who fail the most learn ways to not do things and this inevitably gets them closer to success. This is why we shouldn't be ashamed of our past temporary defeats, failures, and mistakes because if we study them how we should, we will have learned something from it to not do it again. We fail to realize how great of a blessing that failure actually is, it's one of the best things that can happen to us. You may burn your first omelet, you may drop shells in your eggs while cracking it, you may cook it too long, or whatever the case may be. Once we take our focus off of the temporary defeat itself then we can take that lesson from it that we will not keep making these same mistakes. If we keep at it, we can only get better and that's a fact, failure is not meant to discourage; it's meant to encourage; it means we're closer to success.

Kobe Bryant is one of the all-time leading scorers to ever play in the NBA but he has the most shots missed ever. What does this tell you? We all can agree that Kobe Bryant is one of the greatest players to ever pick up a basketball, some even consider him the best but the point is that he shot and missed the most and he also made a lot as well to become one of the NBA leading scorers and one of the greatest of all-time. He didn't let missing discourage him from shooting, you may think he's a ball hog but I'm not talking about basketball here, I'm talking about your life.

Whenever you miss in life, you give up. You stop shooting, you stop living, you stop dreaming and going after your goals. Take notes from Kobe, AKA the black Mamba, because he was relentless no matter what was happening. He knew that over time when he would miss, he instantly thought I'm going to make the next one. Why else would he keep shooting? If you don't think you're going to make a shot why are you even shooting, it's a waste of time; you have to believe before you even take action, that's a must because work without faith is dead before it even starts. It's a fact that you will not make every shot in life, life will knock you down but if you just remember to always get back up and to continue shooting despite what happened in the past, you will eventually fail your way to success. You cannot keep failing if you never quit, it's not possible; eventually, you'll figure success out, you just have to have the stamina to outlast the failures. You have to have such a passion for it that you don't quit when you feel like quitting. When you feel like you've tried everything there is to try, you have to try one more time and then again until you get the results you want.

# YOU CANNOT RECEIVE WHAT YOU DON'T GIVE

Giving what you have and all that you have is the only way to receive bigger and better blessings. Letting go of who you are is the only way to become the person you want to be. Giving opens up the soul for receiving. Most of us tend to hold on so tight to what we already have that we don't allow ourselves to grow out of our comfort zones. This goes from anything financial all the way to things far more important. We should not hoard our blessings, because our blessings are not ours to keep and they are meant to bless others. God gives us everything in abundance; He doesn't run out of anything because The Lord, himself, created it all. We must plant our seeds of blessings and prosperity because choosing not to plant our seeds is actually still planting a seed, only a bad one. Whatever seed we plant, God knows what that is. He knows because He truly knows our hearts. It's not about the amount but it's about the intention and whether we are genuine with our actions.

There's only two people you cannot lie to in this world and that is yourself and the most high. Your giving is a reflection of your trust and faith in God, or lack thereof, and giving is also a reflection of your priorities in your life. People who don't give out of fear of losing something is what controls them and that is not healthy for the soul. The fact that you cannot take anything with you when you die should be a great enough reason to not praise anything material and temporary in this world. I'm not saying giving everything that you own away is the way to your blessings but I am saying that if you fear losing something so much that you can't bless others who are in greater need, then you are not living a truly wealthy life, no matter how much you have for yourself. Giving to others with what you are blessed with is the purpose of living. God put something in you that He didn't put in someone else so that when you two meet you see something in each other that can help one another. God may put things in your pockets, bank account, mouth (gift of words), personality, or talent and ability to bless the world with. Who are we to not give these blessings away to those in need?

Let me explain further. Imagine someone put you in a room full of money and they said you have 10 minutes to pick up as much money as you can, place it in a pile and at the end, whatever is in the pile is all yours. I'll go out on a limb and say most of us would go about this by grabbing as much as we could and setting it down in a pile to go pick up more right? This is how we should do with our blessings but it's not because we are so fearful to lose the money that's in our hands that we won't even put it down to go pick up more. We don't realize that holding on and not giving is actually doing quite the opposite effect of what we really want, which is more. If our hands are full we cannot possibly plant more seeds, it's just not possible.

This is why a lot of people who have nothing and come from the bottom can end up at the top and end up living a wealthy life. When you have nothing it's kind of a blessing in disguise because you have nothing to hold on to that can distract you from planting your seeds that will eventually benefit you. You ever notice how rich people are very cheap? You ever notice how someone who gets rich goes broke more times than staying rich? They forgot what they did to get there; they forgot that it wasn't them being scared to lose something that got them to their blessings. When you don't have anything, you have no reason to be scared to lose; this is why people with nothing have some amazing testimonies about their success in life.

At the same time, their success can also become their failure. When you get something that you're not used to and love it so much that you fear losing it, that may be the reason you will push your future blessings away instead of planting seeds and blessing others to allow these things to multiply. YOU NEVER LOSE WHAT YOU GIVE. You don't lose it because giving is equivalent to planting a seed and what do seeds turn into? More blessings when you're planting the right seeds.

Whatever seed you're planting in your life and in others is the exact tree that you're going to reap; this is just the way life works. You don't plant a seed for an apple tree and get an orange tree, it's not possible. The best part about this is that you get to choose the type of seed that you plant and you have 100% control over this, whether you realize it or not. Every chance you get in life, always plant the seed of life in someone else. Everyone needs a blessing from someone else every now and then; I like to believe we're all in this together. We all know life gets rough and we need each other to get through tough times. If we plant an apple tree seed and we get our apple tree and guard it like our life depended on it instead of planting more seeds from those apples off that tree then what happens? We'll eventually run out of apple trees because we didn't plant more apple seeds from the apples on the tree.

Once our seeds grow into that tree or we get that blessing, it will get so big until it's too much for us to handle on our own that we must give away so that the blessings can continue— it's the way life works. The fear of competition scares us so much that it cripples our ability and practice of giving. Just think if farmers didn't want to sell their products to grocery stores; farmers would be doing themselves and the world a disservice. At the end of the day, we all can eat off the same tree and have plenty to spare so don't hold on so tightly.

Competition is healthy and I'll tell you why. Once we stop being pessimistic about the term, we can get past that and get to what it really means and how it helps. First, I would like to say that your only competition is you. You're a one of one in life and no one can do what you do and how you do it. With that being said, healthy competition is good because it helps you spread the blessings and it will bring out the best creative side of you. I'll use the big 3 car companies for example; Ford, General Motors (GM), and Chrysler. Let's imagine these are the only 3 car companies that exist.

Let's think of the great demand that there is for cars these days; everyone has a car and someone is buying one somewhere every single day in this world. If Ford was all alone producing cars by themselves then they would never be able to keep up with the demand, they would have so much business it would put them out of business. They wouldn't be able to hire enough people and work enough hours to produce however many cars they needed to supply the demand of our population. Can you now see how Ford needs Chrysler and General Motors and every other car company for that matter?

Our blessings are the same exact way, this is why we must share our blessings because they're too much to handle on our own and keep for ourselves. Ford, GM, and Chrysler all make cars but only Ford can make a Ford, only Chrysler can make a Chrysler, and only GM can make a GM. They're all seeds but different seeds and they're all necessary just like all of our blessings that we share with others. This is why giving is so important to receiving. This is the type of competition that helps all parties here; it's a win/win for everyone because everyone has a different seed to plant and that's a positive because all people don't desire the same kind of car.

As long as you know what type of seeds you're planting, you will never feel threatened by competition or what type or size of a seed someone else is planting. One should not have time nor the energy to worry about what others are doing to feel threatened by them. If anything we should learn from each other and share our successes as well as our failures so someone won't have to go through what we had to. I feel as leaders bringing up the next generations, we are to equip them with our experiences and blessings to make it easier for them to eventually do better than us by raising the bar and that's why we must give them what we know and what we have.

One day, I received a letter from my church with the total amount I had paid in tithes and offerings for the year 2014. I had been 100% faithful in my tithes. When I opened that letter and saw the amount, my eyes got very big. I had been more faithful in my tithes that year than ever before and the irony hit me that I made more money and received more blessings that year than before as well. I was overwhelmed with joy and started to tear up because at that moment, God had showed me if you're faithful to him and bless others you will never lack and your cup will literally run over as He states in the Bible.

That entire year up to that point had flashed through my mind. At that point, I had already received several blessings.122114919 Just to name a few blessings: I got my dream car, brand new off the lot with only 10 miles on it, I had moved away from home to my new apartment, I was blessed to bless a friend and take her, as well as myself, on our first trip out the country for her birthday. Two days before I received this letter, I had booked my flight to go back to the Dominican Republic for the second time in less than a year. For my 29th birthday right before publishing this book I took a trip to Europe and visited 4 more other countries. This may not be a big deal to you but it was huge to me and very exciting to say the least but I also realized how much of a blessing it was. Not to mention, I was also blessed enough to be able to bless others, whether it was financially, donated time, an ear to listen, and mentor others as well. In that year, I gave more away than I ever have in my life before then but I didn't even realize how much I gave because our God is so good that I literally didn't miss what I gave. I had never given so much and felt so rich at the same time; the irony, giving really is the recipe for receiving.

God was blessing me so much that it taught me to give with a good heart, because it's not about what, how much, or who you give to but it's more the why are you doing it. The letter from my church was an eye opener, not for me being righteous but for God blessing me with His grace and favor to even be in a position to give. I'm not arrogant enough to believe that I'm in control of everything. I know that I can practice until I become the best at something but I know that God is the one that can create the opportunity for me to be able to put that gift to use. So the fact that you have something to give, whether it's a lot or a little, is always a blessing in itself. I was not by any means always a joyful giver, especially, when it came to tithing; I just didn't understand it. I had come a long way and I have the Most High to thank for that. He never gave up on me. I'm not where I need to be but I thank God I'm not where I used to be. All the glory is His. This literally brought me to tears and the first person and only person I thought I could share this with was my best friend, Don.

I took a pic of the letter from church of my year's tithes and offerings and sent the picture to Don via text message. The text went like this, "Bro, you're like the only person I can share this with who would understand. Just got my total in tithes I paid this year and I'm so proud of myself, bro, not in just giving my tithes faithfully but also the attitude that I've had while giving them. God has allowed me to grow and be a joyful giver, all the glory is his. The Lord has brought me a long way, bro, and it feels so good to give the Lord what's his in the first place. I never thought I would get to where I am today with Christ, bro, he's working on me and I'm not done but just thankful I'm not where I used to be. Thanks for being an example and helping me in my walk with the Lord, bro. God is great, love you, man!"

He responds back with a text message that said, "Bro, thank you so much for sharing. Tithing has been on my heart and mind for some time now. I have been slacking and lazy and not even getting up for church. God is speaking through you to me, bro. I know He is. It's amazing to see your growth and I thank God for putting the desire in your heart because it's all Him that calls each of us to Him for His glory, it's amazing. Thank you so much for sharing, bro, you have no idea how much this helps me, man. I love you too, bro."

After reading the message my best friend sent back to me, I was overwhelmed with joy once again because my reason for sending that message was to thank him for helping me with my relationship with Christ over the last 9 years. He is someone I look up to for spiritual guidance and always will. The way God works in mysterious ways just always seems to catch me off guard. God's blessing to me that day ended up being a blessing to Don. I had no idea about his recent struggle tithing and going to church but God did. It's so funny we never know what someone is going through, that's why what we say and when we listen to people matters more than we know; I truly believe this is why giving is so much more important than receiving. We all have our struggles with different things at different times; no one is immune to adversity in life.

It's so funny because Don was the first and only person I thought to share the news with. The Holy Spirit put it on my heart because God knew and I'm so happy I listened. All the glory is the Lord's; He constantly shows me that my blessings are not mine to keep. When you share your blessings and give God the glory, He can do things that become bigger than your blessing itself. Truth be told, I didn't think my day could get any better after God sent me that message that day through my tithes letter from church but after I shared it with Don and it ended up blessing him, that was a better feeling than my own blessing.

It was like the icing on the cake or hitting a grand-slam in baseball. After that, I instantly knew this was a testimony to write about but I had to wait a day or two to write because I was too excited and filled with joy to sit down and write at the time. To say that I was overwhelmed with joy would definitely be an understatement. It's so much that can be taken from this experience with my tithes. A giving hand will never lack, a closed hand doesn't receive and what's in that hand will eventually be depleted, so give joyfully just for the fact that you're blessed to be able to give in the first place. Why complain if God asks you to give 10% and you have 90% left when some people are not able to do even that, it's all perspective. It took me years to understand the concept of giving or tithing joyfully and that day kind of just summed it all up for me and all the questions I had about giving. It was an "aha" moment to where it all clicked and I now understand what I once didn't just a short time ago; it was a great feeling and I knew I was growing.

I'm not here to tell you what you have to give and to whom or what but I am telling you that if you don't learn to give, you better learn to live a needy life. If you don't learn to let go of things that can be replaced then you'll live a life with an attitude that there's never enough and you'll think someone else can take your blessings, money, significant other, career, or anything else. You'll live in fear of losing everything instead of learning to let go and give. A handful of blessings is never prepared to receive more blessings so learn to pass them out so that more new blessings can come that will blow your mind away if you learn to give the ones you already possess away. A person will never be truly happy and successful until they understand the art and power of giving.

# GREATNESS

*"Success is not own, success is leased and the rent is due
every single day."*

*-JJ Wyatt*

Success, accomplishment, achievement, the list of synonyms
could go on forever but my personal favorite is greatness. It's
something about the word "greatness" that just gives me the goose-
bumps or chills if you will; it's a feeling I can't accurately describe
with words only. But let's not make this chapter about me because
I am a firm believer that success and greatness means whatever it
means to YOU! It can mean the same or different things for different individuals but the most important person is you.

I love the acronym the G.O.A.T. meaning "the greatest of all
time". I believe everyone wants to be great but there are 3 kinds of
people: people who have no idea what it takes to be great because
they just talk, people who know what it takes but aren't willing to

put in the work, and the people who know what it takes and they actually are disciplined enough to do it. You may be wondering what does it take to reach greatness? Well, I believe the most important thing before the work even begins to reach greatness is that you cannot be satisfied with good.

There is a fine line between good and great. The thing about good is that it's not hard to be good at something, you can be good off of your natural God-given ability alone, which is what makes being good dangerous to becoming great. As cliché as it sounds, that will only take you so far because at some level you will get surpassed by the person who works harder than you; a great work ethic will always beat talent if talent doesn't work hard. That's why the most talented teams usually don't win championships because they usually rely on their talent alone and think they are just naturally better than their opponent. It may be true that they're a better team talent wise but that alone is never enough to become great and win a championship. "Greatness never goes on sale." -Eric Thomas. In other words, there is no easy way to get there because it simply takes a lot of time and hard work, point blank. The thing about greatness is that very few people are willing to push themselves out of their comfort zone to see how great they actually can become.

The fear of failure is greater than taking the chance to reach greatness these days but what people fail to realize is that trying and failing is temporary defeat whereas not trying at all is permanent failure; there's a difference. We are all human so it's natural for us, I believe, that when we become good at something, we become content so don't think this is out of the ordinary. Just think for example, if you're the best basketball player on your team or even in the entire city what and why should you have motivation to get better? It's human nature to think that way but people who want greatness don't think that way even if they feel that way; they intentionally plant in their conscious mind that they're never good enough to not need to improve, they don't compare themselves. Your thinking and your feelings should most of the time be on different pages in order to stay out of your comfort zone to be able to grow. At times you won't feel like working out or practicing your craft but that's when your thinking and will power comes in and you know you have to do what you have to do no matter how you feel; your commitment to your principles need to take over at this point. Feelings will come and go and you will never regret that workout or that practice time because you know you want to achieve greatness.

But back to the basketball player, someone who is comfortable with being good will justify to themselves that they're the best player in the area and they already have a scholarship to college lined up so what is really their motivation to work hard if they're already the best? All of what he or she thinks may be true but being great has nothing to do with being better than other people. Being great is maximizing your full potential and being the best you that you can possibly be. Greatness is more of a lifestyle and what you repeatedly do, it's not based on what you've already accomplished. Since no one on this earth is perfect, there is always room for improvement no matter how good or even great you become; you have to stay humble and hungry.

There are no shortcuts to greatness, the road is long, hard, and quite lonely because it's definitely the road less traveled. When that basketball player goes to college they will now be competing against athletes who were all the best players on their high school teams and the level of the game will rise. It probably will rise above them because of his or her poor work ethic; he will have to learn new habits, which is not an easy thing to do so why not create great habits as early as possible. It's a lot easier to be ready and prepared for change than to have to adjust your bad habits. It's never too late to create new and positive great habits for self-improvement for any area in your life. How do you create new habits? I'll tell you what works for me.

First of all, it takes a conscious and constant effort. You have to make a decision every single day to constant improvement because when you decide this, it's impossible to become content and dwell too long on your past achievements or even your failures. Whenever you reach a goal, you may enjoy it briefly but the great ones move on faster than the good ones because they know they can still get better and they want to see how great they can actually become. The secret to greatness is that you never arrive; I'll say that again YOU NEVER ARRIVE.

That's the thing with people who are great, they hardly believe they're great and if they do, they never think they're great enough that's why they're obsessed with practice and improvement because they want every competitive edge they can get; it's almost an obsession that the average person won't understand. People who want greatness are constantly studying, reading, learning, and searching for any new way possible to get better. You have to fall in love with getting better; the process, the journey, the grind, the blood, the obstacles, sacrifices, the sweat, and tears it's going to take.

It all starts with the constant and conscious effort to make the commitment and stick with it no matter how you may be feeling but you have to stick with it. The next thing after making the commitment is that you have to see yourself as you want to be. Don't look at who you are now but have a vision; think, feel, and live as the person you want to become. Correction: the person you're going to become. This habit of thinking and living will have more of an impact than you may realize, even though you may think that thinking is the simplest thing, it's really not. The habit of thinking and feeling as the person you're going to become is no easy task but it's necessary.

I'll continue to say this, it's been proven that it's a scientific fact the way the brain works it knows no difference between you visualizing yourself doing something and you actually doing it. It's all the same to your brain and this is why thinking and having the vision of yourself as the person you will become is so important. With that being said we must be careful what we think and believe about ourselves because it is the power that will influence and shape our lives. We must think and see where we want to be not where you don't and God will handle the rest. "For as he thinketh in his heart, so is he." (Proverbs 23:7)

One of the definitions of "good" in the dictionary is: satisfactory in quality or degree. Satisfactory meaning fulfilling all demands or requirements. Great in the dictionary is defined as: unusually comparatively large in size or dimensions, unusual or considerable in degree, power. I don't know about you but from reading the definitions and comparing the two terms, good and great are not the same. Both are positive but they are not the same. The main difference that jumps out at me is that good means satisfactory, as in fulfilling all requirements. For example, you go to football practice or work and you do everything your coach or boss asks you to do to fulfill the requirements asked of you; nothing more nothing less. Nothing is wrong with this by any means whatsoever, you're doing a good job and I'm sure your boss and coach would love to keep you around. Doing good is definitely a step above average or the masses in my opinion because the average worker in today's society does just enough to get by and not get fired.

By no means is being good average in that sense. Now, the term great says in the definition "unusually comparatively large in size or dimensions". This is saying that greatness takes large and unusual steps to get there; it's more extraordinary or phenomenal. Before I continue, I'll name off some names that will trigger the word "greatness": Kobe Bryant, Magic Johnson, LeBron James, Steph Curry, Jim Brown, Napoleon Hill, Albert Einstein, Venus and Serena Williams, Muhammad Ali, Mike Tyson, Oprah, Beyoncé, Denzel Washington, Eric Thomas, Tony Robbins, Jerry Rice, Brett Favre, Ray Lewis, and many more.

Now, I want you to ask yourself this question, do you think any of these individuals only did what was required of them to get to the level they're at? Do you think Venus and Serena Williams only practiced hitting tennis balls when everyone else was? Do you think Jerry Rice only caught footballs and studied film when the coach told him to? You think Kobe Bryant only shot a basketball while the team was practicing? I don't know any of these individuals personally but we both know that they did a lot more than what was required of them.

I'm sure they put "unusual" amounts of time and effort into their craft in order to reach greatness. This takes years and years of work; going from good to great may be one of the most difficult things to do for the simple fact we that like to be comfortable. When we are good or doing good at something, we get applauded, complimented, and praised and it's very easy to become complacent because no one will ask more of you; only you will do that. When you're good around average people, they make you feel great but that's a lie, you just seem and look great compared to them. The only person that can require and demand more greatness of yourself is you. The uncomfortable thing about transitioning from good to great is that there's no safe zone; it's not a smooth transition because you're risking who you are for who you want to become.

It doesn't matter how you raise a child from birth or how early you introduce a sport or a career to them; eventually, they will decide what they want to do and how good or great they want to be at it. I'll use an example of one of the great ones listed earlier because he said these words himself; it's not just my opinion. His name is Napoleon Hill and this is by far my favorite author of all time. You should read some, if not all of his books; I highly recommend them and know that you'll love them. He's most famous for being a self-help motivational author and speaker. He also practiced law and has done many other things; he is most praised for his philosophy on success.

To me, the most interesting part about his life is not that he became great but it's how and what he was willing to sacrifice to become great. He is probably most famous and labeled one of the greatest writers of all time from his first book "Think and Grow Rich" in 1928. Ironically, one of his philosophies for success is "Do more work than you're paid to do." This is exactly the opposite of good. In the dictionary, like I wrote earlier, good means fulfilling all demands or requirements. He states in his book that if you do more than you're paid to do, then eventually, you'll be paid more than the amount of work you do.

Now let's think about this for a second. Just think of someone who's achieved greatness; think how much extra work they put in prior to their success. To us, from the outside looking in, it may seem like an overnight success but they have years of doing more work than what was required prior to reaching greatness. They were simply doing more work than they were paid to do, in the words of Napoleon or according to the dictionary's definition of great, they were doing an unusual amount of more work than they were required to do. Do you see the correlation here? The tricky thing about going from good to great is that it's easier said than done, of course. Like I stated earlier, you have to risk being good to become great.

Being good is not as hard as it seems; it's a lot of people that are good but don't become great. Reason being, it's easier to blend in versus standing out. Just think, if everyone or a lot of people around you are doing good how easy it is to stay there. Look at something like the cycle of poverty, most people who are born into poverty usually stay in poverty. Statistics will show you that but look at the "exceptions" like Jay-Z, Nas, and Eric Thomas. Just think, if they accepted being good and blending in to their surround-ings, we wouldn't know who they are today. Something inside of them wanted greatness and to be different than their environ-ment. Now, I'm not here to tell anyone what good means to them or greatness individually. I do know and understand that good to some people may be great to others; one man's trash is another man's treasure and I understand all that. All of this at the end of the day is just perception; it's neither right nor wrong, it's subjec-tive to each individual.

I simply believe good is more common than great, not based off someone's abilities but their decision to not become more. Not that we all don't have that potential for greatness but it's scary to take that risk; you get looked at like you're weird or crazy for doing more than you're asked to do, people even criticize and laugh at you. It's simple math; it takes more to get more; you get out what you put in. Just think about how when you do more than asked and people say, "you're an over achiever", "brown nose", "teacher's pet", "suck-up", and "you're wasting your time because it's not nec-essary". Greatness can be very discouraging, that's why there are very few great people and there tends to be a lot more good and average people in this world.

You may be wondering what makes Napoleon Hill's philosophy on success so credible? He not only preached his philosophy of do more than you're paid for but he practiced it long and put it to the test himself before he began to preach it. Maybe you're wondering how long is long? Well, is 25 years long enough for you? I can only speak for myself but that's credible enough for me. As a young man, while Napoleon Hill was working as a journalist for a magazine, he needed to interview someone. He was fortunate enough to be able to interview the great, Andrew Carnegie; one of the most successful and wealthiest men ever.

For whatever reason, Andrew Carnegie saw something very special in the young, Napoleon Hill, and took him under his wing immediately. Andrew Carnegie then asked Napoleon Hill a question that would change his life forever. He simply asked Napoleon was he willing to dedicate 25 years of his life without pay to study and research the philosophy of success and then teach it to the rest of the world. Andrew Carnegie said he would have to find his own means in order to live; he said all he would do is organize and set up interviews with great and successful individuals for whom he could interview about their success.

So Napoleon had to continue to work to be able to support himself. Now, I don't know about you but if I was asked that question by a man I barely knew, whether he was the wealthiest man alive or not, I probably would've laughed or have given him a blank stare that said you've got to be joking I'm only being honest. I'm sure Napoleon thought these things because he said so himself that he doubted it before he said yes and even afterwards as well. Obviously, something inside of Napoleon believed in Carnegie, and also himself, that this unusual amount of time and effort that was to go into this task was worth the risk. That little faith he had was all it took.

Can you imagine the amount of criticism that Napoleon received from his friends, family, and peers? To the extreme of this commitment, I'm sure the criticism wasn't just a laugh; it probably was concerns for his finances as well as his psyche. Like I stated earlier, you have to decide to be great. Most people never understand your actions and reasons at first, until the greatness starts to come about. It's all about delayed gratification.

Being good is common so people see it all the time and know what it takes. If you've never been great or been around greatness then you simply won't understand it. Andrew Carnegie understood it inside and out. At the time, Carnegie was well-beyond greatness so he obviously knew what it would take for Napoleon to reach that level. He was simply trying to pass on greatness to someone else. In Carnegie's auto biography, he credits his success not to what he himself knew but instead to the people what he didn't and did what he couldn't. He surrounded himself with successful people; it was his mastermind alliance and they all were great and successful. I think he picked Napoleon Hill and asked him to devote 25 years of his life to study and master this philosophy on purpose. I think he saw something different in Hill and knew he would be up for the challenge. I think a man as great and successful as Carnegie would not ask just any random person to carry out this life's mission.

Napoleon Hill had never in his life been exposed to someone as great as Andrew Carnegie. Just think, if the Average Joe would've asked Napoleon to commit to this 25-year study, I think Napoleon would've politely said no to that person. With Andrew Carnegie's credibility and Hill being aware of that, as crazy as the offer was to devote a quarter of a century to study something without pay, he knew inside that it would be something worthwhile. The simple fact remains that Napoleon knew that Carnegie was great, therefore, he had to know what it takes to become great.

This is why I think that little bit of faith gave Napoleon all he needed to accept and say yes, despite the more logical reasons he had to say no. Andrew Carnegie believed in Napoleon Hill; in fact, he probably believed in Napoleon more than he did himself. Everyone knows the power and influence it can have when someone else believes in you besides yourself; it gives you the feeling that you can move mountains. Even with Napoleon accepting this 25-year task, it doesn't mean that at some point he didn't have fear and doubts.

Going from good to great involves risks, which is scary and naturally produces fear. Stealing second base in baseball involves the risk of getting thrown out, there's no way around that, but it also runs the risk of reward of making it to second base. The reward of stealing second base without getting caught is that you become one base closer to home plate and scoring a point for your team. This is no different than going from good to great in life with whatever you want to become great at. The risk is uncomfortable and always will be but the reward is everlasting; once you score that point in baseball it can never be taken away because greatness lasts forever. If you do get thrown out while attempting to get to second base, then you live to bat again and fight another day; more opportunities will come.

For whatever reason, we would rather focus our time and energy on what we don't want versus what we do want in our lives. In other words, we would rather focus on the negative instead of the positive. The law of attraction says what you focus on and think about the majority of the time will eventually come about in some way, shape, or form in your life. Trying to change this habit of thinking is very difficult to do, in fact, trying to change any habit takes a constant effort that won't happen overnight.

The society we live in today doesn't help our habit of negative thinking in the least bit. You can go or look anywhere to find negativity from the media, news, newspaper, movies, schools, families, peers, and even churches. The point is that you will not have to look very far for negativity. To find positivity in this world takes effort and it's quite the challenge; becoming great when good is so acceptable is just as difficult. To be great and positive, which I think go hand in hand with one another, requires a lot of self-discipline.

The great thing about self-discipline is that you have 100% control over it, no outside source can conflict with it unless you first allow it to. Self-discipline is simply formed through creating habits and having good reasons for them. There are things like desire, passion, purpose, values, morals, goals, and many more that you need to be motivated to even begin to discipline yourself for what you're trying to accomplish. In other words, you need a reason that means enough to you personally to self-discipline yourself to change your habits for the better. The first things I think of when I think of self-discipline is our health by taking care of our body, and keeping it in top shape because it's our temple. The amount of discipline it takes to continuously take care of your body is extremely difficult but the price you pay if you don't is a lot higher than the cost of discipline; it may even cause you your life.

One thing I've always found interesting growing up in the Midwest where we experience all five seasons to each extreme is our workout habits. By pure observation, over the years I've observed around and after Christmas or for New Year's resolutions, most people set out to make these new workout plans to become healthier and fit. Reason being is because spring season will be quickly approaching and less clothing will be worn so your bodies will be exposed for others to see much more than compared to in the winter months. I'm not saying anything is wrong with this if it works for you, trying to better yourself is always a good idea, no matter what, when, or where. My thing is this, you take a shower or a bath every day and see yourself, you knew what you looked like before making these resolutions, why wait to start when it's about to get warm?

If your only motivation to force yourself to work out and get healthy is when other people will see you then that simply means what others think of you is way more important than what you think of yourself. I don't know if anyone has ever told you this but you're the most important person in the world and if it takes for someone else to cause your self-discipline before you do, then we have a problem. The fact remains that if you were really dissatisfied with yourself, it wouldn't take for others to see you to take action. Any motivation to better yourself is better than none at all but this kind from other people should never be the sole-reason you take action to discipline yourself; it'll never last, I know because I used to be that person.

I see people do this work out New Year's resolution for three months then go back to old habits and the cycle continues and repeats itself every year. The irony is that places like California, for example, don't have this problem as much because it's always nice there and it's always time for a "beach body", if you will. When working out, there is more of an expectation and not an exception, it's a lifestyle there but is it really because of the weather or are people out west just more disciplined? I honestly don't have the answer to that but I would like to believe that we're all somewhat affected by what others think, which can be a good motivation. However, we should not let the weather, nor the opinion of others, dictate our self-discipline.

What people fail to understand is that here in Ohio, winter months tend to make it more challenging to work out; but stopping and starting is harder than just continuing to work out. Once you start doing things for yourself, to better yourself, it's an unbelievable feeling of bliss. When you experience this feeling of doing things for yourself first, whether it's working out or coming out of a long relationship where you've lost yourself, you'll always learn that self-love is the best love, self-discipline is the best discipline, and self-motivation is the best motivation. This is not being selfish but it's hard to do for others when we are not in a healthy state for ourselves first; whether it's to become the best husband or wife or to become the best person at your job or anything else you do with your name on it.

We only get one body so why wouldn't we take care of it all year long? Why would we decide to exercise only 3-4 months out of the year when that's not fair to your body? What if your body's white blood cells, whose main purpose is to fight off any foreign bacteria or virus that you come in contact with to prevent you from getting sick, decided to work only 3 months out the year? You would be one sickly person all the time who would be in and out of the hospital; you wouldn't feel good at all.

The tricky part is that lack of physical activity and the consequences from it, usually don't show until years down the road when we're older. To people who don't work out, this creates the illusion to think they're fine and healthy; maybe they don't like how they look but at the same time they don't feel as if they have a good enough reason for change. This reason also causes the opposite of motivating people to work out and to schedule regular doctor check-ups to make sure everything is okay. If you're motivated by yourself and you don't like how you look or feel, it becomes easier to discipline yourself to work out all year around; it also doesn't take for you to seek other's approval to confirm your results and your commitment to staying healthy. Like I stated earlier, we're all human and I love a compliment just as much as the next person about my body or anything else.

When you do things for you first, you don't seek or need other's approval to get you going and keep you going; they just become bonuses because you're going to do it regardless of what they say. I know after I work out, I feel and look good without someone having to tell me; the feeling is actually more important than the look because it gives you confidence and it's a mental stimulation as well. I don't think I'm arrogant for loving the results of the hard work I put in while in the gym, I think that it's absolutely healthy, as well as necessary.

We all have different reasons and different motivations for working out or striving for anything for that matter, but the thing that separates the good people from the great people is that the greats find a way to keep working at something when no one is looking. When you see a successful person, don't look at what you only see on the outside, do some homework and find out how they go up to this point because the process starts when no one is looking. I'll bet whatever I own that they're working on their craft all-year around and not just when people can see them.

# LEFT OVERS

I 've always been an advocate of the "right now" or the "present". I've learned and I continue to learn that all our blessings are right now or in today, as I would like to say. I preach this message but I often find myself, as many others, not taking my own advice at times. I share this chapter with you as something I'm currently working on in my own life and one that I will constantly practice to get better at daily. I'm just letting you know that I'm human just like you; I have not arrived and never will as long as I'm breathing because there's always room for God to allow me to get closer to him to get better at life. The goal, in a literal sense, is never perfection but to simply get better; as long as you're moving forward and catch your mistakes and bad decisions when you make them and learn as much as you can from them, then you're on the right path.

This chapter is very special to me and I think a lot of people will be able to relate because I think we all battle with patience in some way, shape, or form in our lives. We tend to think what's in our tomorrow will be better than our today. Now, don't take that in a literal sense and think that we all don't have bad days because sometimes we just want to get through and hope for a better one tomorrow. I completely get that we all have our fair share, but I am a firm believer that we are what we repeatedly do and how we think and react to situations that are currently in our lives.

A habit doesn't mean perfection but I think we always tend to lean one way more than the other. I think we all have sinful ways in us but I believe we all have our creator, God, in us as well; the most important thing and what makes you is which one you constantly feed to grow in you that will eventually come out of you. That's how you end up who you are; we all have flaws, sins, and imperfections but which way are we constantly going? That is what I mean by who we really are, not what we are in a sense that we are imperfect beings, because we all are.

I usually go to the gym after work when I get off at 330am, this was a Tuesday and when I got off work I did just that. Usually, when I go to the gym that late or early, if you will, there's usually a few people in the gym with me at the most. Well, this day there was no one there except me, myself, and I. It was also after one of those long days at work and my body just did not feel like working out, so my feelings at the time were conflicting with my decision to stay committed to working out. Never let your feelings over power your will and decisions to commit to something no matter what it is, big or small, that will become a habit.

Of course, I worked out like I always do and always will as long as I'm able, but while working out, I just felt God's presence in the gym. In between sets of working out, I was talking to God out aloud since I had the gym to myself; it was just Him and I. I asked Him what did he want me to do today, how could I serve Him and serve others by letting Him use me. I asked Him to enlarge me to his higher calling and that I'll only work for Him and not man so what was my mission. I think it's funny how sometimes we get answers from God instantly and sometimes it seems to take forever. A relationship with God can be frustrating because everything is on His time which is always on time, but we want things on our time.

I can't speak for anyone else but I have a lot of growing to do with my spirituality and relationship with God, so when I feel the presence of the Holy Spirit, very clearly I ask as many questions as I can and find ways to obey what it's trying to tell me. If I have access to write the message down, I will stop what I'm doing and jot it down; if not, I'll put it in my phone. If I'm at work, I'll repeat what God is telling me over and over until break time and put it in my phone; I sometimes had to do this for up to 2 hours before a break at work. I find that it's always worth it because whenever the Holy Spirit is present, it serves a purpose that's bigger than myself and I couldn't live with the fact if I didn't listen to God when he spoke and missed out on an opportunity to bless someone who needed it.

I always pray for God to put in me what others need from me. When I say need, I don't mean in necessity or in a literal sense but need as in we all need each other to grow in life; we're all connected in different ways through God's plan. We all have gifts, talents, and abilities that need to be shared with others and vice versa. I believe this is what life is and ultimately what it is all about. The closer we get to God, it will bring us closer to others in our lives to help them and for them to help us.

All things work together even when we can't see it or notice it, with that being said, I first needed to apply it to my own life before I began to preach it in this chapter. Right now, I am currently working at the Toledo North Assembly complex (Jeep) factory. I am an assembly line worker; it's a great job and I work with great people. It has great benefits and I have no complaints at all. It's a job that you can live comfortable financially and, eventually, retire from and live a good life. That is all good except for me, personally, this is not the job I will retire from and I know that by my faith.

God called me to serve a different purpose as far as a long-term career in my life; not to say that where I am is a mistake because there's God's work to be done exactly where I am right now. If you notice, I didn't say better because we're all designed for specific things in life and I was just created for a different calling which is becoming a firefighter, author, and motivational speaker. Even though this is not where I will remain long-term, that doesn't mean that for the time being I'm not where I'm exactly supposed to be right now and that doesn't mean it doesn't serve a purpose that will enable me to be better and more equipped for my future endeavors.

In the Bible, in Matthew 14:16, they came to Jesus and only had five loaves and two fishes to feed thousands of people. Most people know or have at least heard this scripture where Jesus performs the miracle and multiplies the loaves and fishes to feed everyone while having some left over to spare. After they ate and fragments were left over, as it says in the bible, God told them to gather up the left overs and when they gathered them all up, it ended up being 12 baskets full. People tend to tell me I'm an over thinker, whatever that means, and maybe I am but let's think about what does it mean and why they gathered the fragments after they were already full?

I compare this to when I was a kid growing up and my mom didn't like for us to waste food; she would always say that it's people in the world who don't have food. Now that I'm older, I reflect back and think that maybe not wasting the food wasn't about me; it was about others. Nothing should be wasted, let alone food. Your food and your blessings can be of help to someone else; what we think is waste are actually fragments to be packed up and taken, even if we don't know the reason it may serve in the future.

I'm at Jeep right now and it serves a purpose; it's no less important than when I become a firefighter, public speaker, and an author. I actually think Jeep is more important because it's where I currently am at the moment; I'm not a firefighter yet so I can't leave the Jeep (fragments) behind or think it's of any less importance.

People often say to keep your eyes on the prize and I don't believe there's anything wrong with that but we often forget that the prize isn't always at the end; in real life, we don't even know when or where the end actually is. The food you eat now or the situation you're in now will have left overs, experiences, or blessings to take with you that will grow on you for your next phase in life, closer to your ultimate goals, if you will. In fact, the fragments left over may not even be for you; they may be to bless someone else for their future so don't worry about if you're not hungry, pack up all of the left-overs in your life and take them with you. The situation you're in now may be for you to bless someone else or inspire them to what they were meant to be.

I think we overlook the little things in life too often to the point that we begin to chase happiness or our blessings. We tend to forget that all of our current blessings are the ones we need to get us to future blessings; it may not be all the ones we want but God knows us better than we know ourselves so trusting in his timing and wisdom is crucial to our current happiness in life. It's like saying after Jesus fed the thousands of people and instead of packing up the fragments, which ended up being 12 baskets full, they just left them there. When we become no longer full in our current state, we tend to search for the next meal or blessing when in all actuality, the small fragments and blessings that should've been gathered would've made up another entire meal in itself.

We tend to forget that all big things are made up of a lot of small things; big things don't just happen, it takes a consistent effort in the little things to arrive to bigger blessings. In the bible, in Luke 16:10, it says, "He that is faithful in that which is least is faithful also in much; and he that is unjust in the least is unjust also in much." In other words, God has to trust us with small things in order to trust us with the bigger things because bigger things come with more responsibility, that's just how life works. "For unto whomsoever much is given, of him shall be much required." [Luke 12:48]

One of the biggest leftovers in my life is football, which I'll talk more about later. I played football from the time I was 8 years old until I was 23 years old so we're talking 15 years of my life here. Football was a father to me; it taught me so much from hard work, discipline, how to lose, how to win, being punctual, to be a team player, and most importantly, it taught me that life will have its ups and downs no matter what but how you respond to them is what's most important. I took all of these morals and values from football and took them into the real world and into the workforce when I started working jobs after college and after pursuing the NFL.

A lot of things that were natural to me from football helped me tremendously when working all of my jobs; working hard, showing up early and leaving late. To me, this was natural because this is what it took to win football games but you realize when you get in the real world that these simple values and type of attitude are not popular with the masses. These things will separate you from the Average Joe who comes to work a few minutes before he or she will be late and do as little as possible just to not get fired. My leftovers from football and what became normal for me allowed me so many new job opportunities and promotions that I really couldn't believe it. I never felt like I was doing anything special, I was just doing what I felt like I was supposed to do and that's my best, treat everything the same, show up first, out work everybody, and be the last to leave.

Football taught me that the competition was never the man standing across from me, but instead, the competition was the person I saw in the mirror; he was the only one that could stop me. Life and football go hand in hand and I'm a firm believer in that. My leftovers just happened to be football but what are yours? Think about all of your past experiences that helped to mold who you are today. Think about all of the jobs you worked, all of the people you've met, your support system, the way you were raised, your education, and everything else in between. These things make up who you are in the next phase of your life; when you look at someone's past it can most of the time pretty much explain why they are who they are today and that can be for better or for worse depending on how they use their leftovers.

# THE PRICE OF SUCCESS

D o you put a price tag on your dreams? If so, why? How much is it? How much is too much to pay for you dreams? I've observed that people constantly complain about the price of things. We complain and complain some more when in reality, if you want anything in this world, you'll have to pay for it. It may cost you a little or it may cost you a lot but it's going to cost you regardless if you like it or not. That's just a part of life, no matter how you cut it. One thing I'm learning is that when we pay for something, it's either a purchase or an investment. The definition of a purchase is to acquire by the payment of money or its equivalent; buy. While the definition of an investment is the investing of money or capital in order to gain profitable returns, as interest, income, or appreciation in value.

With a purchase, you get exactly what you pay for and when you invest, you're more so planting a seed and will reap the benefits later; there's a return. I like to think of it as an investor is the farmer who plants and grows the crops and the purchaser is the person who goes to the grocery store and buys the farmer's products. I think this analogy correlates to so many things in life, including our dreams and our success. Before my words are taken literally, I want to say we ALL are purchasers in life, that's inevitable, from our clothes, cars, food, houses, or anything else, we all are making someone else richer by buying their products. Nothing is wrong with that, that's part of life and how it works.

Unfortunately, we all are not investors; being an investor is a choice, one can be a purchaser all of their life and never become an investor. To be a farmer/investor it takes what a lot of people shy away from and it's called "work." As the great Thomas Edison said, "people often miss opportunities because it comes dressed in overalls and it looks like work." This is the reason purchasing is so much more attractive than investing. Same reason that lusting after a beautiful woman is more attractive and easier than building a relationship and a lasting marriage. Looks are so deceiving and they always fade with time once you really get to know someone.

While the purchaser gets something instantly in return for their purchase, an investor gets nothing but work and labor in the short-term. The tables turn when the seasons change; the purchaser bought the farmer's/investor's products and now the purchaser has to work more to replace the money he used to purchase things while the investor is sitting back collecting the benefits from their investing. This gives the investor leverage and options because the investor can invest or reinvest in his business, ideas, dreams, or the investor can go purchase things if that's what they desire to do.

I look at it like a slingshot, if you want to shoot a lot quicker and not delay then you don't pull it back as far but when you shoot it faster, it won't go as far or be as powerful either. If you want your shot to go farther and be more powerful then you pull it back farther, which the tension builds and it gets harder to pull back; the effort is worth it because your shot will always go further. That's the difference between investing and purchasing. Investing is a minor setback for a major come up. The farther you want to go, the more you have to invest; life will give you exactly what you put into it. Our success is a reflection of the work we invested behind closed doors.

I'm starting to learn that it's really nothing wrong with success. Why do so many people become successful and remain unhappy? It's the value that we put into our success and accomplishments that's the problem. If you don't know the value of yourself before you accomplish anything, big or small, you will not be happy and if you are, it won't last. We seek an infinite comfort in temporary things. Love who you are and what you do more than what you get out of what you do and how people treat you based on your success. When you know the true value of yourself, you cannot be sold or bought at any price; you have the leverage and you will keep it.

I'll use two of my favorite celebrities for examples; Hill Harper, as I've talked about earlier and Dave Chappelle. Hill Harper graduated from Harvard Law School cum laude, but with his passion being acting, he turned down all kinds of six figure lawyer opportunities. Not to mention being thousands of dollars in debt from getting that education, but he had a passion to become an actor. He sacrificed and became a waiter at night to have a flexible schedule so he could go to auditions throughout the day; what a humbling transition. (I am not saying there's anything wrong with being a waiter/waitress, just the transition from Harvard Law School to becoming a waiter by choice is abnormal.) I say that to say that no matter how much money law firms were offering Hill, he couldn't be bought because it's not what he wanted to do. He knew what he wanted to do, he knew the sacrifices he had to make and he was okay with that.

The rest is history, Hill Harper is a great actor, a best-selling author, and motivational speaker making more money than he would've ever made as a lawyer. Not that how much money he make is the most important thing here but I truly believe when you follow your passion whole-heartedly money will always follow. His story is inspiring, all because he knew his self-worth and couldn't be bought out of what he really wanted to do; money had nothing to do with the value of him and his dream. As for Dave Chappelle, having the amount of success he did in comedy and walking away from a $50 million contract to continue his show makes you wonder two things: what could have been that bad that he walked away from all of that money and you have to really know the value of yourself to even be able to turn down that kind of money. Some people even may think he's crazy but I don't; I think people are crazy who are controlled by money, not the other way around. I have nothing but the upmost respect for Dave Chappelle and his decision because most people aren't that strong to say no to money the way that Hill and Dave did.

If you are willing to do anything and everything for "success", you lose your values, morals and you give other people and/or things the opportunity to control you whether you realize it or not. Please pay attention to what I'm saying and not what I'm not saying. I'm not saying money, fame, success, accomplishments, and dreams are bad things because all of the above can be used for good to better your life and be a blessing to others; all I'm saying is that you cannot lose who you are for the sake of having these things. If you don't first accept God's love, which is unconditional and self-love, you will seek what you're missing from the lack of those two in other things or people. That's why some successful people with everything they've ever asked for seem to be so miserable.

No person, place, fame, money, accomplishment can make you content, fulfilled, and at peace like The Lord's love. There's no comparison and honestly, me writing this does it no justice because it's just something you have to experience first-hand. The funny thing is that God's love is and always will be there, we just simply have to accept it; it's that simple. The closer I get to Him, the more I'm at peace and have true unreasonable happiness. I'm not saying I don't have goals, dreams, financial goals, and all of these things because I actually probably have more than the average person; they motivate me daily in their own way and that's not a bad thing, I don't think. God wants us to stay hungry and seek improvement in all areas of our lives because if anything matters than everything matters, but he also wants us to remain full (content) with his love and the blessings we already have.

God's love is the only thing any of us will ever really find true peace in because it's the only thing that's for sure and always will be. Just think when you accomplish a goal, what do you do? Make more goals, right? It's an ongoing and never ending process. I've learned and I'm still learning that accomplishing my goals don't define who I am or make me valuable. I feel like none of my goals hold the key to my happiness, but my happiness is the key to my goals because one who only accomplishes a thing can still feel something is missing. So much goes into a goal that I think we forget that you don't have to wait to be happy.

Whether you fail or succeed, neither one is permanent and life always goes on. If you enjoy the short ride we have on this earth then you'll start to see how everything you went through is for the better. The person you are isn't permanent and where you're at is exactly where you need to be to become all you can be. You're the person that God made you to be and that's a one of one, which makes you successful and a blessing in itself. Just stop reading and say, "Thank you, God, for making me *me*." Everything else is just a bonus or icing on the cake, if you will.

Your goals, talents, and blessings are not yours; they're not meant to make you feel good or worthy or valuable, that should already be a given because you're YOU. In my opinion, our goals, dreams, talents, and successes are meant to bless others, period. What other purpose should they serve? Life is designed for us all to win and we must keep this in perspective. If you don't accept God's love and love yourself, it's hard to put others before yourself and truly help or love them. It's easy to love when you know you're already loved by the Most High and yourself. It takes faith in The Most High to know that he will always take care of you so you must help others who may need your blessings or the gifts that you possess; that is why we are blessed with talents, money, and success to give and share it with others.

I know that no matter how "successful" I become or how many things I accomplish, it could never make me more valuable than I already am. Nothing in or of this world could ever add or take away from being a one of one, you're the blessing; not what you do or don't do or become. Keep this in perspective and all of your successes and failures will never make or break you. They will help mold you and bring you up and give you more options but they can never define who you are.

Some people wait their entire lives to achieve a goal or dream to feel worthy and I think that's a horrible way to live; to me; that's counterproductive. Please do go after your dreams with all you have when your heart desires to do so but please enjoy the race while you're running it. You don't need to cross the finish line to know you're already a winner. You should know your worth by the preparation that you put your blood, sweat, and tears into and who the Lord created you to be long before you even start the race.

It's so funny how we chase the big things when in reality, we can only find joy in the small things within the present. Never let anything in the future hold your key to your happiness hostage. I cannot drive this point home hard enough, there's nothing wrong with progress or wanting bigger and better things out of life; there is a problem if we remain unhappy until we get those things. I correct my last sentence, if we "think" those bigger things will make us happy then we are only fooling ourselves.

We have to keep life in perspective at all times because being needy and always wanting is the fastest way to unhappiness. We want a better and high paying job when the one we have now pays our bills just fine and there are some people that don't have jobs at all. We want a new car when the one we have works just fine and gets us from point A to B just fine with a low car note or it may already be paid off, so this car is saving us money but we want a new one. Nothing wrong with wanting a new car but the sad part is that most of the time we don't even want a new car because we want it, we want it to keep up with the Jones.

We all get caught up in this at times, I believe; it's really a part of human nature. We tend to forget that the smallest blessings are the best blessings, what we have is always more important than what we don't. There's nothing wrong with buying a new car, like I said, but that's not the point I'm trying to make; if we don't appreciate what we already have then no matter how much more new stuff we get, it will never be enough. We will continue to chase a fix that cannot be fixed. I think our consumption problem is pretty equivalent to a drug addict. A drug addict is forever chasing the first high they experienced while we're constantly chasing that temporary feeling when purchasing something new. We keep buying more new things because the feeling never lasts. It just becomes something you constantly chase that you cannot catch;

things only run away from you when you chase them, including and especially, happiness.

Happiness is something you attract not chase; real "unreasonable happiness" as Hill Harper calls it, comes from within you. The only power we don't possess within ourselves is the power we give up. We can give up happiness, that's why a lot of us aren't happy. If we are not first happy with who we are whether it's the bad, good, or indifferent then we will never be happy no matter how much we have. Happiness really is simple and so is life, but simple doesn't always mean easy. I think we even sometimes make things harder than they need to be by trying to find some magical solution to happiness. It's all about consciously and constantly staying focused and keeping things in perspective. Focus on the positive and not the negative; give all of your time and energy to the things you want to attract and accomplish in your life. Keep in perspective that where you are and what you're going through is never as bad as it seems. Always remember someone would be blessed to have the struggles you have.

I once read a quote, "If we all put our problems in a pile then we all would rush to pick our own back up." I love this quote and I think it's so true; it's always about perspective. In the Bible it says you should ask for what your heart desires and it shall be given if you believe. [Psalm 37:4] God wants you to want and seek what you're heart desires, that's a great thing. What I think there is something wrong with is complaining about what you already have and where you currently are. My thing is why complain? There's absolutely nothing it can do for you, it will not get you out of where you are now and it will not help you get to where you're trying to go. Complaining is like going to the gym but not working out; it's a waste of time.

# DATING

I don't like dating. Dating is very necessary and it has its seasons and its reasons but I do not like dating. I've come to realize, learning a lot about myself over the last few years, that I'm just a commitment kind of guy when it boils down to it. I have not always been this way, although, I'm still a work in progress. I've matured and grown in more ways than one and this just happens to be one area that I've improved in. At one point in my life, I thought I could date the rest of my life and I never saw myself being committed in my near future.

I had to look in the mirror and be truthful with myself that I was emotionally unavailable when it came time for commitment. I would basically draw a line when I would date and that line was not to be crossed no matter what. I knew I didn't want what came on the other side; I came to find out what was on the other side was commitment and I was not ready for that. I was this way for years and it took me to read my fellow fraternity brother's book, "The Conversation" (by Hill Harper), who I'm continuing to reference throughout this book to realize that I didn't want to be this way forever. After reading his book, I had to do some research and learn about myself. I always believe when there's something you want to fix about yourself, you have to learn why you're doing the things that's getting the results that you wish to change.

I'm a firm believer that we are creatures of habit and something molding our habits consciously or subconsciously comes from parents, experiences, peers, family, religion, school, values, morals, TV, social media, and the list is endless. I think it takes courage to go back to your past and revisit some things that maybe weren't so pleasant to begin with; things that basically made you who you are today but you know revisiting them is necessary to get to where you want to go. I believe until you accept who you are, you cannot become who you want to be. The only person that can get to the root of the reason you are how you are today is you. Can you imagine how hard it must be to be a psychologist? They're professionally trained and skilled at getting to the root of people's problems and they usually can find out what that is but that's not the difficult part; the difficult part is getting their clients to face reality and deal with it to work on it.

It has to take an extremely patient individual to work with people like that on a daily basis. Dealing with people who sometimes either don't know what their problems are or don't want to face them. Just think about it, we all have that one friend or family member who comes to you for the same advice over and over whether it's about their toxic relationship or leaving that job they hate to pursue their dreams. You constantly give them the same advice over and over again but they continue to make excuses and they keep doing the opposite of what you're saying. They get frustrated with the same results and come right back to you again then they wonder why you don't give them advice anymore. As cliché as it sounds, you cannot help someone until they want to help themselves and you cannot truly help someone until you figure out why they do what they do. What about their past experiences that has made them into the person they are today?

As I faced my past about being emotionally unavailable and not being interested in dating, I had to respect my past, yes, I think we must respect our past for better or worse and I think this is very important. Wherever you are in life at this exact moment, you made it; you're still alive and breathing, which means you've survived. Even though we may have habits we want to change, the habits have gotten us thus far so let's respect our past in that sense; I think this is very healthy and necessary for us to do. We all know that just surviving isn't good enough because we want to live the best quality of life as possible, whatever that may mean to you; hopefully, it's to be successful, happy, healthy, and wealthy.

Without me realizing it, I believe that my lack of interest in dating started to come about when I started truly committing to other things. We all know that going through high school and college, we think we know everything and we believe that we have the world figured out and our future planned ahead. We know what we're going to do and when we're going to do it; I don't say that to say that we can't accomplish these things, I believe we just don't know the commitment that it takes to achieve them. After graduating from college and experiencing the real world, those next five years changed me in more than one way for the better.

The biggest change was that I started self-educating myself more than I ever had; I read hundreds of books, biographies, auto-biographies, self-help, and anything else I could get my hands on to better myself. I was committed to self-improving and this changed my life for the better. I found out that life is just like a relationship, you can't have a successful marriage without being committed. If you're not committed to your spouse then when hard times come, the relationship will not last. When you get married, you have to continue to date you're husband or your wife, you have to constantly work on what got you up to that point of marriage. There is no difference with our dreams and goals in life; if you're committed and make a vow to never quit going after what you want in life, then in due time, with a lot of hard work and adversity, you'll eventually get what you want.

As I started learning and studying other's success stories, it made me take myself and my dreams more seriously; I became committed to everything that I wanted out of life. I knew that to get where I wanted to be, it was going to take everything in me that I had; all you have is your best and your best is all it's going to take. The irony was that I was so focused on self-improving and committing to my dreams that dating someone or being in a committed relationship was literally the last thing on my mind. Come to find out, while in the midst of being focused on me and my dreams, I was simultaneously creating a new me when it came to dating and relationships.

I was making a new standard for myself when it came to dating; if we aren't committed or working towards that then let's not waste each other's time. I learned to value my time so much that wasting it was never going to be an option, so I literally had no interest in dating. I've come to learn that if anything matters then everything matters so it's hard to balance being committed to one area and not committed to something or someone else in your life. You may get along living in such a way but your life will continue to be out of balance as mine was because whatever or whoever you're not committed to it will always show; everything in the dark will come out in the light.

You can be successful at work but if you're husband or wife isn't happy because you don't put the same efforts in with him or her like how you do at work, then you will be a success at work but a failure at home. In my opinion, home is more important because that's where you lay your head and raise your family. The situation goes both ways, even if you're happy at home and miserable at work, that's not good either. The goal is to be balanced and be committed to all things that you're a part of; don't give less than 100% to anything that you're a part of because you will not get everything out of something that you don't put everything into.

If you want the blessings and to achieve your dreams, you have to be willing to endure the stresses so commitment is the most important part of this journey of life and everything else in between. Speaking from personal experience, it's a lot easier to stay committed to someone or something and work through the problems than it is to keep starting over. Starting over may paint the illusion that it feels easier because the beginning of something usually isn't the hard part. It's when things are getting tough and the only thing that keeps you from quitting and giving up is the commitment itself, that's the real test and that's what allows you to grow and overcome any obstacle life can throw at you. Then and only then will you become unstoppable and achieve greatness once you commit because just dating or being interested will only take you so far.

# PRE-APPROVED BLESSINGS

We all are what I like to call "pre-approved" for our blessings in life. In the eyes of God, everything is already done and has already happened; time does not apply to The Most High. With that being said, this is the perfect way to exercise our faith in him because if we truly believe and expect our blessings before we get them then that is feeding our faith in the Lord and building our relationship with him. When you are pre-approved for something, we all know that means you've already qualified to get whatever it is that you want. This applies to God and how he blesses us. We tend to get caught up with if we live "good" or "righteous" then we should have a good, easy life and receive many blessings; when we or others live "bad" then we shouldn't expect any blessings at all and bad things will happen, "karma" if you will.

I think one of the most often asked questions about Christianity and life in general is why do bad things happen to good people and why do good things happen to bad people. Well, for starters, good and bad is nothing but perception of what you think and how you react to what situation that is put in front of you. The other thing I think we fail to realize is that there is not enough good we can do to qualify for our blessings and unconditional love from God and there is not enough bad we can do to disqualify us from his love and blessings.

We are always qualified for our blessings, not because of our righteous living but because of God's unconditional love and His perfect grace. Every decision, for better or worse, that we will make in life, God already knows about it; everything is mapped out and already played out from His standpoint. We have been blessed with free will so we always have a choice to choose whatever it is that we want to do in life but when God blessed us with this free will, I think he knew at times it would be too much for us to handle. I believe that God knew that in order for us to have hope and faith in Him, His love would have to be nothing less than unconditional; He knew all the bad choices we would make and He decided that He would always be there no matter what.

This is the only love of its kind, nothing on earth can match the magnitude of it. Marriage doesn't even compare to it; I mean why do you think you say your vows before God? It's because it takes God to be the center of the marriage to keep a lasting marriage; how God loves us is the perfect example of how you should love your spouse because things can and will get ugly on some days more than others.

Our relationship with God is there to remind us when we may not like our spouse that God never gave up on us so we shouldn't give up on the one we committed to before Him. That's why marriage cannot and will not last without God in it. We are too imperfect and selfish to love someone unconditionally with our own strength and abilities. We are emotional creatures, we react a lot off of how we feel, and when we do good unto others, we expect the same in return. As we all know, that will only exist in a perfect world because people are going to take advantage of you, even people that love you and unfortunately, that's just a part of life. People take us for granted but we tend to forget that we take God and his love for granted as well; he loves us with perfect grace and has never left us alone or done any harm to us yet we seek others love for confirmation in our lives.

We seek material things, we can't let go of relationships that aren't healthy, we feel worthless without our dream job, and the list goes on. Nothing is wrong with these things but the only fulfilling thing in this world is God's love;122114919 He loves us because He created us, He knows us better than we do, He knows our wants and desires but most importantly He knows our needs. He knows that our needs are not what we always want and seek but as they say, patience is a virtue and God has infinite patience with our imperfect ways of living. He never leaves or gives up on us but we don't always realize how much of a blessing this really is.

I like to compare being pre-approved for our blessings with the purchase of a new car from a dealership. We all have ourselves or know someone that has purchased a new car before and it can be a long and frustrating process that can really test our patience. If you don't get pre-approved for your loan before you go up to the dealership, it makes it a longer process because you don't know if you'll even get approved and how high the interest rate will be.

To the contrary, if you go in the dealership already pre-approved then you know you're going to get a new car, you know how much you're pre-approved for, you have a whole new confidence about your-self because you simply know what's going to happen. You're not asking anyone for anything but instead you're telling them what already is. This is no different than how we live life based on our faith; the more faith we have, the more we know and expect our blessings to come. The less we have, the more we are like that person going into the dealership blind not knowing what's going to happen.

The ironic part about it is that at the end of the day, the person who got pre-approved and the person who didn't might even end up with the same exact car when it's all said and done. What is the one difference in the two? It's the journey they took. Was the journey made harder than it needed to be for the person who wasn't pre-approved? I like to think so, the journey to buying a new car and the journey in life to our blessings is far more important than the destination; how we embrace and have faith in our journey will be the center of our happiness or our misery. The more faith we have in God to trust the process and the journey because we know we are already pre-approved for what is coming, the better our lives will be.

We can have fun and not worry about the bank approving us or denying us that loan for the car. We know only The Most High can open or close doors of opportunities, not a bank. The comparison to the bank approving us for that loan is the comparison in life by us basing our joy and happiness on other things and other people. If you go in that dealership and you're not happy until that bank approves you for that loan for your new car, then the fact remains you were not happy before you got the car and you will not be happy after you purchase the car. Eventually, your high off buying the new car will fade away. There's nothing wrong with buying a new car, that's not what I'm saying, but placing your happiness on that new car is definitely a problem. If we are pre-approved for that new car, we know we're going to get it and it's just a matter of time. How can we apply this to our everyday lives while chasing our dreams, goals, success, and happiness? We have to find a way to live with such faith to know blessings are going to happen, claim them, and speak life into them on a daily basis because we are indeed pre-approved.

When you want something in life, you have to not only work for it and toward it but you have to also prepare for it. Those who prepare for their blessings are ready once they get what they were praying for. People who prepare for the blessings expect them to come; it's an expectation. Those who sit, wait, and only hope something happens feel like their blessings are an exception when they end up happening. Life will push you around if you let it, but life will also be submissive to all that you desire if you take a stand.

Life cannot hold you back, only you can hold you back. Our lives are nothing but a reflection of what we believe we can achieve. We just like excuses; we like to give our power away, claim we've been dealt a bad hand and can't do more than we're doing. We blame our parents, race, financial situations, lack of educational opportunities, gender, and whatever else because the list is infinite. We all have excuses and at one point or another we have all used them in order to rationalize not bettering our situation. .

We link more pleasure to procrastination than we do to putting in the work to be successful. We link pain and pleasure to the wrong things and we wonder why we aren't successful or happy and we wonder why others are. There's no secret to the fact that you get out of something what you put into it. People who call other's success luck are people who are failures. If there is a such thing as luck, I believe the harder you work, the luckier you'll get and luck is nothing more than preparation meeting opportunity. If you think someone else's success is because of luck, then you better get to studying their techniques. There's no secret to success because it takes a lot of discipline, faith, and hard work. Some people only work hard when they feel like it; they don't have the discipline to work hard all of the time in everything that they do despite how they may feel. It's not easy but it's possible and it will all come down to how bad you really want it.

To be successful and get those blessings, you truly have to enjoy what you're doing more than what you're getting out of what you're doing. I always like to say and try to live by, work hard not for results but work hard because it's the only way to work. With this mindset, you won't seek rewards just because you work hard, you're working hard because you love what you're doing. I'll also add that your work ethic and habits are a reflection of you and your self-brand, whether it's true or not it will say a lot about you. Now, I'm not saying I don't like rewards or recognition for my hard work but what I'm saying is that it cannot be your primary motivation; it won't last because it cannot sustain alone.

Praise and rewards come from others and I don't care how good you are, eventually, praise will turn into criticism. I mean look at all of the greats who were loved and admired at one point and hated at another. We can't seek validation for our good habits from others, it shouldn't take for someone else to approve your actions. What's important is that you know what you do; you know your intentions for why you do what you do and with that alone, happiness should be found in between the two. Others actually understanding what you do and why you do it should just be a bonus; their recognition should not be expected nor taken for granted either.

Thank people when they speak highly of you but don't be surprised when they no longer speak highly of you; you have to have a purpose that's bigger than you and someone else's opinion. This is how we live a successful life and have a peace of mind to live life to the fullest of our potential. Expect your blessings because they're already pre-approved.

# WHAT KIND OF CAR DO YOU DRIVE?

The reason you don't have what you want is because you settle for what you don't want. The reason vision is so powerful is because what you want may not be in front of you so you seeing it in your mind may be all you have at the time; what we often times fail to realize is that that is more than enough. What we want is greatness and extraordinary and nothing less than success but some of us don't have any examples of this in front of us. You're used to seeing average all around you, you're used to seeing a Ford Focus but you want a Mercedes Benz. The hardest part is not getting comfortable with anything less than what you want; if you want a Benz don't settle until you get exactly that.

Some of us act like we want something but we don't really believe we can have it, we don't think we're worthy of a Benz. We just hold on to that Ford Focus and hope, wait, and see if it's actually possible to get that Benz. If you want that Benz, you have to get out of that Ford Focus mindset. No one is going to bring you a Benz, you're not going to win it in a raffle, you're not going to hit the lottery because you have to GO GET IT. You have to put all of your focus and all of your energy toward working for what you really want.

It may take months or it may take years but keep your focus on exactly what you want; don't worry about what everyone else has, don't worry about what you're driving in the mean time because none of this matters. Once you have that vision of that Benz, when you get in your car that you have now, use your imagination and imagine you're in that Benz; keyless infrared start, sitting on that leather, gripping that stirring wheel with that famous emblem in the middle of it.

Your imagination is more important than you know; go back to being a kid imagining everything you want and work towards that. Kids have the perfect imagination that adults need to go back to because somewhere along the line, we became so "realistic" and stopped imagining things. If we really knew the power of vision and imagination, we would not grow out of this as adults with the masses. Once I learned that it's a scientific fact that our brains don't know the difference between using our mind to imagine and something actually happening in real life, I started taking advantage of it. Believe me, it works; I have experience with this.

I was driving a 2000 Dodge Durango when I decided I wanted a new car and well, my Durango broke down so I went to a dealership and tried to get something brand new off the lot. The one dealership I went to denied me because I had no credit built up so I couldn't get exactly what I wanted without a co-signer and I refused to ask someone else to be the co signer. They then referred me to a used car dealership who would work with me. Ultimately, I ended up getting a 2008 Mercury Milan and it was a good, clean, and nice car but it wasn't what I wanted, it wasn't "my Benz." I drove that for about a year and one day, I saw the most beautiful car I'd ever seen that became my dream car; a 2014 Dodge Rally Redline Challenger. Once I saw it, I had to have it.

From the moment I saw that car, I got a picture off the internet and made it my screen saver on my phone so I looked at it every single day. When I got in my Milan, I pretended that I was driving a Challenger, even though I wasn't but in my mind I was. After this ironically, I just started seeing so many Challengers driving around the city. You will attract exactly what you think about the most and focus on according to the law of attraction.

I went on the internet to see what dealership had that specific color, year, and model Challenger that I desired. The next day, spur of the moment knowing my credit wasn't up to par yet, I decided to go to the dealership and said I'm not leaving here without my Challenger; I had already picked out the name for my car (Pepper Mint Patty). The salesman asked me did I want to look around and see what I wanted and I told him that I wanted a particular car and showed him the picture of Pepper on my phone. He said, "I'll have to check and see if we have it in stock." I said, "I know you guys do." He then said, "Okay I'll get the keys." Took it for a test drive and the rest is history; I am now driving my dream car without a co-signer, not a lease but I own it; it's my baby.

This story may not be inspiring to you but let me further elaborate. This story is 100% true and everything in it is accurate but this is not actually about a car, I'm talking about your life! Are you driving the car you want in life? Are you living your dream, your passions, or are you only accepting only what life offers you? Are you passively going through life on auto-pilot hating your job and just working to get a paycheck just to pay bills? Are you scared to start over and do what you really want to do? Read these lines very carefully; life is an aggressive contact sport, you have to demand what you want and work hard until you get exactly what you want.

It's going to take a vision, it's going to take time, it's going to take sacrifice, it's going to take even more hard work but time is going to pass anyway and you can fail at something you don't want so you might as well fail going after something that you do want. Stop driving a Ford Focus, GO GET YOUR BENZ or whatever it is that you want! It's not coming to you, you have to go get it and never settle for anything that looks like it; you deserve better and you can have it if you take action. Be thankful for what you have but never stop working towards your goals to get exactly what you want.

# LEADING AND FOLLOWING

*"If serving is beneath you, then leading is above you."*

*- Peris DeVohn*

I truly believe for one to be a well-rounded, healthy, happy, and successful individual we must learn to embrace that we have to be great at both leading and following. I won't go into the discussion whether leaders are born or made but I think on some level, we all are leading someone whether we realize it or not. We also all have role-models and follow people to strive to be like them; hopefully to be better. It's important to know who you're following as well as who's following you. Never follow someone that you would be upset if your life ended up being like theirs.

People say you should surround yourself with people who are doing "better" than you. I don't like the term "better" but I get the gist of it. Surround yourself with people who are constantly challenging you and themselves to be better in all aspects of life. It's so true that "iron sharpens iron; so a man sharpens the countenance of his friend." [Proverbs 27:17] Choose to follow people who have experiences you don't have, who grew up differently; in other words, find people who can bring things to your life that you can't and you can also bless them with your blessings as well. You don't even have to have a personal relationship with the people you aspire to be like.

Hill Harper likes to call these people your "board of directors". If you don't know by now Hill is clearly someone I aspire to be like. Hill Harper is my #1 role model and the one person who I aspire to be like in almost every way. I've studied him, read his books, and I've done endless homework on this great and successful man. He was even a factor on why I joined my fraternity, Alpha Phi Alpha Fraternity Inc. I've even had the pleasure of meeting him when he came to my city and did some motivational speaking; he also inspired me to become an author.

He's the most humble and down to earth person you'll ever meet; that conversation changed my life. I don't have a personal relationship with him but he is a role-model to me. I'm sure he's aware of the magnitude of the impact he has on others with his success, he's a very smart guy so I know he knows but not all leaders know this and accept the responsibility.

Some people know it and see it as a burden; it's too much pressure but great leaders embrace this responsibility and become conscious of their actions because they know they can literally change someone's life for better or worse by how they live theirs. They realize that their life effects more than just them and that God blessed them to be in this situation to help and lead others. This doesn't mean they're perfect nor do they try to live perfectly, they're just aware that when they make mistakes, they admit it to their followers so people won't make the same ones as they did.

Any leader that tries to appear to be perfect isn't a leader, they only care about their image and not the people who are looking up to them. Leadership is a circle because just like how I view Hill Harper, someone views me the same exact way. It may or may not be on the same magnitude but that doesn't matter because leading one person down the wrong path as a leader is one too many and leading one person down the right path is success in itself. Knowing who you're influencing is a leader's job to figure out and we must realize the truth that someone is always watching.

I will forever be a student in this game we call life. The more I know, the more I realize I don't. It's a gift to be able to teach and not everyone has that gift but we can all learn. We can all become a master of something, hopefully, that something is our own life. Being an example is far more effective than having to be labeled a "leader" to be able to teach someone who's following you. Words sometimes get in the way; words are often misused when your actions are not lined up with your intentions. What and how you live often doesn't need to be explained if one's image and character are the same.

If you're always you then you rarely have to explain yourself because you never take a break from being who you are and, eventually, people will accept you whether they like it or not. If our image is not aligned with our character then you're not giving people a chance to choose you as a person; this is robbing you of your gift of being you. To make someone love you and become infatuated with your image is just prolonging them to getting to know the real you and what's in the dark will always come to the light.

We all want to be accepted but we must first accept who we are before anyone else will accept us. We settle for people liking our image rather than our character and this leads to superficial happiness, which goes away when people go away. There's a light in you that's meant to shine and give others light; you don't need to get them to look, they'll see it if you let it shine and use it to bless others. The more you know the less you have to say, the more you learn the more you'll realize most things don't need to be explained; either you get it or you don't.

People either want to know or they don't. What you're dying to teach someone, you won't have to if you're living it because they should just be able to look and observe your life and learn it. This is the power we hold by just being us and the magnitude of the influence we have on others goes beyond our understanding. Our life is like dropping a stone out the sky into the ocean, the ripple effect of the impact keeps going beyond our sight but just because we can't see it, doesn't mean it's not happening.

Good leaders help others when they make mistakes in life but great leaders do everything in their power to prevent the people who look up to them from making the same mistakes that they did. We should not abuse the power of leadership; one must not become comfortable with just correcting other's mistakes. We must realize and be real with ourselves as leaders that we're not going to always be there to save the day so we must think of long-term solutions rather than quick band-aide fixes with people who look up to us. We must prepare them not to depend on our help and wisdom but to depend on themselves; that should be the ultimate goal as a leader, nothing more and nothing less.

Another important quality about being a leader is meeting people where they are. Once you become a leader, it's no longer about you and this is why great leaders are so rare, important, and special. It takes a great individual to constantly be there for others because a lot of things that come easy to leaders are things that are difficult for others, therefore, leaders may spend a lot of their time teaching things that are second nature to them. Leaders may get frustrated with this because they're humans but they expect and accept the challenge because they know it's not about them. They must meet people where they are and not be concerned with having to leave where they are as leaders.

Leaders don't lead from the front; if you're too busy to make the time to help others, you're really not a leader and you just like to be in the front. If someone looks up to you for whatever reason, it's your job to leave the front, go back wherever they are, and help them no matter how easy whatever they're going through is for you. Leaders don't lead from the front, they're always available for wherever they need to be for the people they need to help.

# WE LIE MORE THAN THE DEVIL

We all know and have probably used the expression "the devil is a lie" at some point in our lives". I can only speak for myself to admit that but I have used the expression quite often. The idea did hit me to reconsider this statement. I'm not saying it isn't true but I am merely looking at it from a different perspective now. I've learned and I'm still learning that when adversity is present in my life, that I must always look in the mirror first for the start of the problem and begin working toward a solution. I am taking the same approach to "the devil is a lie" statement.

I believe that the devil is better at deceiving than lying. Some of you may be thinking lying and deceiving are pretty much the same thing but it's not. The devil knows God better than we do; he knows our blessings in life are coming. He knows the truth, but the more important question is do we know the truth about God's plan to prosper in our lives and the blessings that are coming? Do we know the truth and do we also believe that God can make the blessings become a reality? To call the devil a liar, I think, subconsciously places the blame on the devil to take away our power of choice to believe him or not. A lie that's told and not believed has absolutely no power.

The devil knows our weakness and will try to exploit them at any opportunity he has and he knows by him just planting the seed of doubt, it will eventually lead us to start believing his lies. If we had no doubt in our minds and all faith in God's truth, any lie becomes irrelevant. The fact remains that the closer we are to God, the more we listen to his truth, begin to live it, and get away from the devil's deceit, the less relevant the devil's lies will become in our lives.

Misery loves company as also the devil does, too. Let's not forget the devil experienced heaven at one point and got kicked out. When you lose something good, you naturally don't want anyone else to have it; in other words, the devil wants some company. The devil has to deceive us because he knows he represents bad and that's why he must dress up his lies (deceive) to attract us toward his lies and get us to fall for temptation; otherwise, his tricks wouldn't work on us. He makes his deceit look attractive but when we sin, which we all do, the only reason it happens after we know better is because we make the choice to lie to ourselves to justify what we've done; it's what we tell ourselves that makes us take action, good or bad.

The moment we rationalize our sins and lie to ourselves is the moment the devil's deceit was successful. We must remember that we lied to ourselves by using whatever excuse or rationale to go against our principles, moral, and values to commit a sin. The devil cannot tell you that lie, only you can. The devil doesn't lie, he deceives; we lie, then we sin. The devil knows the truth but we often times don't; we lose sight of the truth and faith in the Lord but that doesn't make it any less true than it already is. That fact always remains in place and we lose sight of that before the devil does and as we do, that's when the devil uses anything and anyone to get us to lie to ourselves and become distracted away from The Most High's truth.

Our number one enemy is ourselves and the devil uses you against you to lie to yourself after you already know God's promises for your life. If we know God's truth and hold on to it, whether the devil lies or deceives, what difference does that really make? It wouldn't make a difference, which is my point. That's why the devil masters the art of deceiving because deceit will get you to have doubts and to lie to yourself which is far more powerful than the devil lying to you.

I told you the devil is smart; I mean think about that, he knows how powerless he is and how mighty our God is that he knows he has to first get our focus off God's truth to even have a shot at deceiving us. A lie is only as powerful as much as you convince yourself to believe it, would you agree? Just think of a situation you've been in when someone is lying to you and you know they're lying but they don't know you know. I can't speak for anyone else but it's hard not to laugh in that person's face as they continue to lie to you and because of this, their lie holds no power.

A lie is only as effective as the person it's being told to; the liar and the lie holds no power if they don't believe it. Now, we may not always know when people are lying but when it comes to the devil, we always know he's lying, I've never heard someone say, "the devil speaks the truth." Lies from the devil only possess as much power as we give them; that comes in forms of fear, self-doubt, failure, insecurities, lust, and the list goes on. Therefore, the devil uses deceit to make us think those things are true even though most of us know that doubt isn't real and that none of us are failures;

that's perspective and we truly have nothing to be insecure about because God created us all to be special.

The deceit from the devil will cause you to believe the negative thoughts. No one will be absent of negativity and negative thoughts, no matter what but the key is to not feed into them. Don't become consumed in negativity because it's a trap and don't forget the Lord's truth and plans for you to prosper no matter your circumstances. "No weapon formed against me will prosper." [Isaiah 54:17] They will form but they will not prosper because we are blessed coming in this world, as well as going out. Don't wait for something to happened to count your blessings; you're blessed because of who you are, not from what happens to you. The enemy can only take your happiness if you allow it.

# DEFEATING THE ENEMY

To defeat the enemy, you must know your enemy. When a boxer trains for a fight, each fight is different. Training involves studying his/her opponent's weaknesses and strengths. If you know your opponent well, it allows you to work smarter and not harder because strength means nothing if you can't apply it and use it effectively and efficiently. Life is no different than boxing, you must know yourself as well as your opponent. In life, the devil is your opponent and fear is his weapon of choice. Your strength is you but you must first know your opponent's gameplay before you can make good use of your own strengths to work in your favor.

Fear is not a bad thing; fear is only bad when we fear it and let it control us. Fear is a normal emotion for us but for whatever reason, we've made it out to be a negative thing. If and when we face our fears, the devil cannot use them against us. The devil is much like a bully; once you stand up to them, they'll leave you alone because they know they can't control you by fear and intimidation anymore. They don't like resistance you can't bully someone who fights back whether they win or lose because then it's no longer bullying, it's a fight!

As a firefighter, we are taught that fire likes to travel where there is least resistance. When we open a door to go in a structure that's on fire, we've created what's called a flow-path. We're feeding the fire oxygen to keep burning and we're creating a path of least resistance with an opening for the smoke, fire, and hot gases to flow toward. In other words, studies show that you're walking into the flow path as you created it by opening the door so it's inevitable that until you knock that fire down, it will be coming toward you in due time. The devil acts just like a fire, he only uses fear on people who don't fight back with resistance and face their fears with faith; faith is the only way to fight that fear. This is why bullies pick on people who don't fight back; bullies don't want to fight; they just use fear to pick on people who are afraid to fight them back. In other words, they are cowards and rely on fear to fight for them; they look for the easiest route possible just like fires. The devil tends to travel and work just the way fires do.

We have to come to the realization that we are in control. Once we understand that we have the power then the devil becomes powerless. We are not looking for the absence of fear in our lives but we are looking to use it to our advantage instead and learn to master facing our fears. I always like to say if I'm not scared and uncomfortable with my dreams and goals then they're not big enough. In my opinion, fear is a clue that you're on the right track. The devil uses fear as a way to keep you from going after your heart's true desires. We are so scared to take a chance and go after our dreams that our fears paralyze us to the point we're scared to try and take action, then and only then is when the devil wins; by keeping us from even trying.

We don't feel worthy and we fear failure but what we don't realize is that successful people fear failure also but they just at some point decided to have more faith than fear to take action. Whatever you fear failing at is what you need to go towards. We fear love and going after our dreams more than anything else. The devil is great at making the good things in life seem scary and impossible while making sinful ways and things more attractive, easy, and pleasurable. The devil knows when we don't feel safe and we lack faith and that's when fear will take over if we let it. We all have fears and always will. All of us also have faith but which ever one we feed the most will have the greatest impact on our lives and be the reason for our quality of life.

You ever wonder why sin, lust, lying, and anything that's not healthy for our mind, body, or soul is easy, feels good, and is comfortable? This is the game the devil plays. He makes the bad appealing and makes the things you need to do to set yourself free scary and fearful. I cannot say this enough, we must go toward fear; that is the right way and the only way to live your true purpose in life.

There's stories of mothers who lifted cars by themselves due to the fear of their child dying. Fear is a strength that we can channel and use to accomplish anything. If the mother would've let the fear paralyze her and not take action, then the child probably would've died. This is what happens when we let fear control us from living our true purpose; our dreams will die when we don't take action but if you try then you will accomplish all you set out to do as long as you never quit because if there's a will, there's a way.

While playing sports in high school, I never understood the real importance of studying my opponent and learning their strengths and weaknesses. It wasn't until I got to college that I finally realized how important watching film was. In college football, you're going to either love to watch film or learn to hate it but either way, you're going to watch film and a lot of it. In sports, as well as life, the higher you get in competition, no matter what you're doing, the competition will get tougher. Doesn't matter if it's from high school to college and on to the professional level, the thinner the line will be that separates success and failure. I've always prided myself into working harder than my opponent and any other competition but I wasn't enlightened on working smarter as well as harder until college.

When I got to college, just about everyone was my speed (not really but everyone was a lot faster versus high school), stronger, quicker and the competition was just on another level. The talent and skill level evens out, unlike high school where you're most of the time just the outright better player compared to everyone else as far as talent alone. In college everyone is talented or they wouldn't be there; they were one of the best, if not the best player on their football team in high school. Something will separate you from the next player and that may be who's working harder, as well as smarter. I was a defensive guy and I learned very quickly that talent and the physical aspect is only 10% of the battle in football while the other 90% is mental.

When you play defense, it's harder because you're reacting to what the offense does. This is where studying your opponent and watching film helps a ton. If you study your opponent to the point you know where they're going before they get there, this will make you a great player on defense. If you ever watch a great defensive player, they seem to know the offensive plays before they happen. This comes from hours of studying their opponent and their tendencies on film, it's not just a lucky guess. Studying film is like building a relationship with someone; if you're around someone and pay enough attention to them, you will naturally pick up their habits and tendencies.

Have you ever been around an old married couple that seems to just read each other's minds and complete each other's sentences? It's a beautiful thing to witness and they're the type of relationships that last because they know each other so well. Getting to that point takes effort and time. Knowing someone that well can also be used for bad as the devil gets to know us because this is what he uses in a negative way. He learns us, learns how to tempt us and with what; he knows that fear will keep us from achieving greatness, not because we're not capable or incompetent but because it causes us not to even try.

That's what studying film does; you learn the other team's strategies, habits, tendencies, and anything else that can give you an edge. The film never lies and film is always great odds to play by. Your own past is film to study on also, how you let the devil defeat and discourage you, or it's film on how you defeated him. If it's not broken then don't fix it but with every new thing we set out to do, there's always a new devil waiting. For this reason, we must never stop studying film, because we will always have an opponent.

Faith is simply the courage to face fear without actually knowing what or how things will turnout. As I stated earlier, there is no way to completely get rid of fear but that shouldn't be the goal to begin with because fear often brings out the best in us. Fear is nothing more than an energy and an emotion that's neither good or bad until we decide how we will use it or let it use us; it will define how it's empowering and motivating us or if we're "choosing" to let it hinder our happiness and success.

# PRIORITIES

The moment you make happiness a goal and not a priority, it becomes out of reach. We must understand that to be truly and genuinely unreasonably happy, one must make his or her happiness a priority instead of a goal that you're chasing after to attain. I'm not saying anything is wrong with goals because they're great they keep you focused, motivated, and headed in the right direction. There are many things in life that we should have as goals but in my personal opinion, happiness should not be one of them. The reason I say this is because a goal is more external, something outside of oneself that you're trying to accomplish or attain. Like I said, this isn't a bad thing but making happiness some kind of goal is giving up your power and your right to choose and decide to be happy from within.

A priority is something in your life that you make time for and you always make it happen because of the importance you give it. You make your priorities happen by any means because of what they mean to you, not because it's necessarily easy or convenient. The best part about priorities is that we have the ability to choose our own and the order in which we put them. You don't have to go to work, you choose to. You don't have to pay your bills, you choose to. Do you pay your bills or pay yourself first?

These are things that only end up the way they end up by the decisions we make whether consciously or subconsciously. (Not making a decision is also making a decision and not making a decision is the worse decision you could ever make.) If your priority is to pay your bills before you pay yourself then that will play a major role in how you treat money and how money works for you or you work for it. It's a mindset but it makes all the difference in the world. We always hear people say we never realize what we can do until we're actually in the position, well, I say that to say if we make a priority to pay ourselves first before we give then you'll learn to adjust and live by those priorities by any means. Life will be better because you're controlling your money and it's not controlling you but that's another subject.

I always laugh when people say they don't have time for things like going to the gym to work out, building relationships, quality time with family, reading, or going to church. I purposely say those things because growing physically, mentally, spiritually, and socially and keeping them all balanced is most important to a happy and healthy life. We all have the same amount of time in a day to use, no matter how much money one has or doesn't; we all just choose to spend our time differently on different things. Money cannot buy us time but prioritizing can maximize our time to get more out of it. Whatever is important to you, you'll make time for it regardless, so my question is why would we not make time for our own happiness and make it the ultimate priority?

It's the craziest thing about people that I don't and never will understand; we'll go to extreme measures to make time for everything else. We'll go to extreme measures to make money; we sacrifice our time, family life, sleep, marriages, and everything else to make some extra ends but yet we push our happiness to the back end of our priorities like it means nothing. We'll sacrifice the people and relationships that motivated us in the first place to gain something that you've always wanted but they loved you before you even had it in the first place.

It's quite insane if we truly think about the tradeoff of the things and people we give up to make money and money is just one example, the list is infinite. We continue to push our own happiness back like it means nothing until we accumulate all these "things" and realize that they cannot keep us happy; we claim we did it for others but in the midst of trading off all of our time for money we, abandoned those we were trying to provide for in the first place. Then after that, we still go about being happy the wrong way and by attempting to pursue it instead of just living and being it. You have to know who you are to be happy with where you are and with what you have, whether that's a lot or a little; an attitude of gratitude will take your happiness to a different altitude. Everything inside of you is all you need to become anything you want to be; you are born with this, it's not something you achieve with age or maturity, you've had it all along you just weren't aware. YOU'RE THE ONE!

Make a promise to yourself that you will never let yourself down. The priority of your well-being should be your ultimate priority. Your health is your wealth which means it doesn't matter what or how much of anything you possess if you're not healthy to enjoy it and share it. If you're not helping you then you're not in a position to do something that's even more important; help others. To even be in a position to help someone else is a blessing in itself. Whether that's with money, time, sharing experiences, and/or just giving an ear to listen because at times that may be all someone needs. It really doesn't take as much as we think it does to help someone, all it takes is to first make time and at that moment to put their well-being before your own.

That does not mean abandon your own well-being but at that time just let it be 100% about that person that you've committed to helping. As I've stated, helping others should mean you've already helped the most important person, yourself, not that your life is in perfect order. The fact that you know you need to try to be in a position to help people when the opportunity presents itself, that alone should motivate you to work on yourself. With that being said, it should be impossible to genuinely help others without helping yourself simultaneously.

What's ironic is that taking the time to help others usually ends up blessing the helper as well as the person who's being helped. Their situation may open your eyes to the point that you soon realize you have no right to complain; things could be worse like the person you're helping or their strength may give you strength. Whatever you lack or think you lack, someone has been living longer than you with less than what you have and being happy while in the situation and not complaining.

To become 100% dependent on yourself is not as easy as it may seem. First, before you treat yourself well and better than anyone else ever will, you have to know the true value of who you are as God's child. You were created in His image with a purpose that's bigger than you can imagine that will leave this world a better place if you first believe and work to live up to your calling. If you're not proud, confident, and embracing yourself and your unique life, the good, the bad, the securities, and the insecurities then you will not be able to effectively treat yourself as the most important person in the world that you are. I'm not talking about "self-esteem" in a sense of you "feeling" good about yourself. I'm talking about a true genuine and healthy self-love; this is way more powerful than feelings alone, knowing who you are and being proud of it without anyone ever having to tell you first in order to believe it.

You don't need a job, a spouse, friends, family, boss, co-workers, or anyone else to reassure you of who you are and your worth. I'm not saying I'm against people speaking life into us and encouraging us because we all can use that from time to time. I just think it's very important to know who you are first before anyone else tells you because if you know who you are, you'll know why you're here, what you will do, and what you won't do because you know where you're trying to go and you won't sacrifice that for anyone or anything.

# THE VALUE IN YOU

Once you're secure in who you are, only then can you add to someone else's life, which I think should be our overall goal. Lack of self-awareness is a recipe for ignorance and self-destruction. To not know the power, gifts, and blessings of oneself then you can never experience true wealth. You don't pay for wealth, there's no cost, it's more of an investment; you get a return for your time and effort. The blessing of who you are, what you were made for, and to share it with as many people as possible is the only road to a truly wealthy life worth living.

To acquire things has no comparison to investing in another human being. Our words used, actions put forth, time spent, thoughts and prayers used to uplift others is the ultimate bliss of this thing called life. Only when we work within ourselves to build a foundation to live for a purpose that's bigger and outside ourselves, can we truly leave our legacy here on earth.

A good long-term investment goes further than a well-intended purchase; if you can buy it, it won't last. If it's invested then it lives forever, even after you're no longer here. People invest money so their money can work hard and make their money make more money; if you invest in people's lives then that creates life to give life. You invest in them and they'll invest in someone else and it becomes a never ending blessing because when you genuinely help people with no ulterior motives, they tend to want to help others so the cycle continues.

Once you truly realize the value in yourself, you'll come to understand that no one can compete with you. I'm not saying this from an arrogant or cocky standpoint but it's based on facts instead of an attitude, per say. The reason people are in so much competition with one another is because everyone's definition of success is the same. This is the biggest lie there is and the fastest way to being unhappy. The media and internet will try to show you what they think you need to have or accomplish in order to feel successful but that's all a lie. Your success is the gift you're blessed with to give the world and that is inside of you, no one can give that to you or take it away; you can't earn it, it's yours before God even put you on earth.

Success is not what the world or anyone can give you, it's what you can give to the world and others. Not one person in this world can take what's on the inside of you without your consent. If we focused more on improving what we already have versus focusing on what we don't, we would all be better off. We fail to realize that improving and being thankful for what we have will lead us to the things we don't have. With this mindset, success or happiness never gets outside of us. The irony is that we already have possession of that exact thing most of us are chasing or that the media is "selling", it's all just a matter of choice as to whether we realize it or not.

Stay in your lane, as some people like to put it and stop worrying and comparing your life to other people's lives. Focusing on someone else's life requires you to take away focus from yourself and when you stop focusing on yourself, you forget about your own self-worth. Also when you compare your lifestyle to another person's and feel you're not successful and they are, always remember someone else is looking at your life and thinking the same exact thing about your life; perspective is so important to the point it's everything. Your self-worth is priceless and cannot be bought with any amount of money, fame, or achievements. Knowing your worth is not only important but it's most important because it allows you to control what you can control.

Your gift of you being you is what makes whatever job you're doing important. Jobs, money, and everything else will come and go but you'll always have you no matter where you go or what you're doing. People who are truly happy and successful realize this and this is what gives them the ability to be happy and have a peace of mind in any situation. This doesn't mean everything is perfect because adversity doesn't discriminate but they don't connect their worth and value as another person would with their current situation or circumstance. Whether it be good or bad, they know every situation is just a season to learn from and prepare them for the next blessing.

When successful people win, they enjoy it but they didn't need to "win" to know that they were already a winner. This is how and why they remain humble and hungry during success. I read a quote that said, "When you lose, say nothing, when you win, say less." Let other people judge you by your wins and losses because that's what people are going to do regardless; some people even get paid to critique others, the so-called "experts". The key is to not allow yourself to become that person who judges yourself nor should you judge others this way.

Don't get influenced and get a big head with the praise that comes with winning and don't get discouraged by the criticism that comes with losing. The fact remains that winning and losing are temporary and inevitable in life and there's nothing we can do about that. This should go without saying but the goal should always be to win; you only play to win but the results will be what they will be as long as you give everything that you have, you can always take something away regardless of the outcome.

What we can do something about is how we handle winning and losing. My college football coach at Miami University used to say something that sticks with me until this day; "It's never as good as you think but it's never as bad as you think either." He would say this every single time before we would watch a film and he would critique our performance, whether it was practice film or a game film with all the defensive backs. I used to cringe at the fact I had to watch myself make mistakes on film and be critiqued about it in front of everyone. It took me becoming a little more mature and developing some thicker skin to understand what my coach meant by saying that.

I tend to learn things when I'm able to use them to apply and relate to things in daily living and when I got into the real world after college, I finally understood what my coach meant. What he was saying not only applies to football but to the real world; it's never as bad as it seems and it's also never as good, meaning you can always get better but you're also a lot better than you used to be or think you are at times as well. No one likes to be criticized, we all like to hear how good we're doing but we all know that constructive criticism is necessary and the best way to learn from our mistakes. What I was failing to realize was that our coach was critiquing our performance and not our character or who we were as people.

For a long time, I couldn't separate the two because I was linking my value as a person with my performance on the football field, which was not good. This is the same thing I've been telling you throughout this chapter not to do; don't get caught up in the "wins and losses". I know not to do this from personal experience. I didn't get this out of a book I read or a video I watched; whether my coach told us good job or do this a better way next time shouldn't have mattered and I never had a valid reason to take that personally. My self-worth and the value of myself wasn't where it needed to be at the time. Like I said earlier, you should know you're a winner and a person of value before you win but you should also know you'll never be good enough to stop practicing and being coached to get better. This goes for everything in life, football just happened to be my personal teacher for this important lesson.

When you know the true value of who you are, you can't be bought and you learn to never settle for anything less than what you want. There are more people who don't know what they want than those who do but those who do know what they want, first know who they are as a person. Knowing yourself is the first and most important step to discovering what you want. It's not an easy thing and as simple as it sounds to get to know yourself, it takes a lot of humbling and humility to get to the root of who you are; I know this from personal experience as well.

One must deal with all of their past experiences, mistakes, bad decisions, failures, childhood conditions, mistreatment from others, as well as you mistreating others. You must first deal with these things before you can get that dead weight off of you that's been holding you back to become all that you were meant to be. Time doesn't heal anything if you don't first accept what's done is done and first forgive yourself, as well as those who have wronged you. Learning the value of yourself not only allows you to treat yourself better but it makes others treat you better also. When you know your worth you don't feel threatened, jealous, insecure, envious, or any negative feelings toward anyone else to make you mistreat them. When we mistreat people, it's usually for a couple of different reasons; they mistreated you or they have something you feel you deserve.

Once you get to a certain level of self-love, you learn not to stoop down to someone else's level and once you value yourself enough, you will understand God would never give someone else a blessing that's yours; The Most High doesn't make mistakes. Life is going to happen, people will mistreat you and take advantage of you at times. Don't let how others treat, you change you, it sounds simple but it's difficult and it's also possible. The key is you should love yourself so much that you only allow for that specific person to do it that one time. When people show you who they are believe them the first time because anything after that is your own fault.

One must also never be brought down to the level of wanting to seek revenge, I know this is also easier said than done. Seeking revenge is a waste of time and energy, as well as waiting around to witness "karma" and acknowledge the fact that they got what they had coming because of what they did to you. This is just flat out stupid; we have to have something else better to do with our time than to focus on a person that we claim we no longer care for. If we remain this way, this shows how little we value our time and who we are as people. Wasting that negative energy on someone who's not worth your time could be blocking you from your blessings; we block our own blessings when we don't realize it and it's not other people, the power of choosing what to focus on has more of an impact than we realize.

If you blame others for where you are in life, you're verbally and psychologically giving them power over your life. You're giving them control over you with consent; freedom is a state of mind and if you convince yourself that others have that power then you'll never be free to dream, live, be healthy, successful, and unreasonably happy. Accepting and then deciding that you're the most important person in the world to your happiness, health, and success is the best thing you'll ever do for you. This is the first step to freedom and 365 days of happiness. This and only this will guarantee you a peace of mind to do and become whatever it is that you want to become in life.

It takes God and a village to help you along the way from the Lord showing you favor and others investing in your success BUT it all starts with you. If one doesn't help and invest in themselves and feel worthy of what they desire then there is nothing anyone can do for them on this earth; God, himself, will only open doors for us that we still have to walk through. You cannot ignore yourself and reach out for others to help you, it doesn't work that way in the process of becoming great. Look in the mirror for progress not perfection but always look with honest eyes, not the expectations of others. To truly love yourself whole heartedly you have to know yourself. Once you start to treat yourself great, you will stop tolerating mistreatment from others and giving their thoughts, words, and opinions so much power over you.

"Death and life are in the power of the tongue." [Proverbs 18:21] I live by this principle if someone, be it family, friend, peers, loved one, co-worker is not speaking life and life only into my life then they cannot be in my life. You don't have the right to have any of my time if we're not helping build each other up and helping one another grow and learn. Words are more powerful than we realize, words carry the power of influence and I know what kind of influence I want around me. I know I can't control what people say so I just control the people I'm around.

All of my relationships in my life are win-win relationships; we both give and receive. No, I don't measure who gives what and how much, that's petty and not important but what's important is to be able to give without worrying about being taken advantage of and being able to ask for something without feeling ashamed. These are the only people that are allowed in my life and I do not feel guilty about that at all, so sorry I'm not sorry.

Back to the scripture, if life and death are in the power of the tongue then whose mouth do you think is most important? Your own, of course. You're with you 24/7 365 days of the year so you listen to what you say and think all of your life. Whatever you say, you had to first think it and whatever you think will come out; thoughts are just as important as words.

There was an experiment on professional athletes from track and field for them to literally think through and envision themselves starting, running, and finishing their entire running event while just lying there. These athletes were patched up to monitors and machines for the study while they literally just sat there and "meditated" through their event. Shockingly, the studies showed that the brain and the body knows no difference between thinking something and actually doing it as I've stated earlier. How cool is that? The power in the choice of our thoughts. We all know that words have the most influence on what we think and eventually become so we must protect our own right to live, dream, think, act, and achieve. If we don't exercise these rights on a continuing basis, on a level of consciousness, then outside influences are what will run our lives; it will be a system doing all of your thinking for you.

To allow someone else to do the thinking for you is easy, it takes no effort. It's staying in your comfort zone and not challenging yourself and the world to grow into who you're meant to be. When you allow the system and others to do the thinking for you, before you know it, you end up 40 or 50 years old and very unhappy at your job that you chose for the wrong reasons and that you constantly complain about. You complain about how you hate coming to work but you never mention that you're choosing to do it; you say you have to do this because you have to pay this or that. Once someone feels they have to do something aside from the fact that they choose to, they're no longer thinking on their own because they're mentally a slave. Whether they're doing it for the money, job security, benefits, or they're just comfortable and afraid of change, this is what not being a person in control of your own thinking will get you.

It's like a hamster running on their wheel, they don't even know why they're running, they're just running because it's there and their master put it in the cage. There's no destination and no feeling of self-worth but when you don't think outside that box then you only utilize what's in the box. A person who does their own thinking cannot be talked into anything they truly don't desire, they have a vision and a laser focus on their own goals they've tailored made for themselves. Now, they may have to wait and work some jobs (no job should be below you that's not what I'm saying) they may not like before they get there but their vision is their motivation. Their vision is always on their mind and they're always thinking long-term when their situation isn't where they would like it to be at the time.

# BIG THINGS VERSUS LITTLE THINGS

It's so funny how we chase the big things when in reality, we can only find joy in the small things that are present. We should never let anything in the future hold our key to our happiness hostage. I feel this goes without saying but I'll still say it; there's nothing wrong with progress or wanting bigger and better things. The Lord says it himself, we were meant to live in abundance. However, there is a problem if we remain unhappy until we get those bigger and better things. I correct my last sentence; if we "think" those bigger things will make us happy then we are only fooling ourselves. We have to keep life in perspective at all times to the best of our ability because being needy and always wanting is the fastest way to unhappiness.

We tend to forget that the smallest blessings are the best blessings; what we have is always more important than what we don't. There's nothing wrong with buying a new car, that's not what I'm saying, but if we don't appreciate what we already have then no matter how much more new stuff we get, it will never be enough.

We will continue to chase a fix that cannot be fixed. I think our consumption problem is no different than a drug addict and their addiction. A drug addict is forever chasing that first high that was experienced while we are constantly chasing that temporary feeling when purchasing something new.

We keep buying more new things because the feeling never lasts. It just becomes something you constantly chase that you cannot catch because it doesn't exist. The irony is that things only run away from you when you chase them, including happiness and success. Happiness is something you attract not chase, real "unreasonable happiness" as brother Hill Harper likes to call it, comes from within by living your passion and putting all of your gifts, blessings, and energy into the world to make it a better place.

The only power we don't possess within ourselves is the power we give up and decide not to use. We give up our own right and choice to be happy so that's why a lot of us aren't happy. If we are not first happy with who we are whether it's the good, bad or ugly, then we will never be happy no matter how much or what we have. Happiness really is simple and so is life but simple doesn't always mean easy. I think we even sometimes make things harder than they need to be by trying to find some magical formula to happiness and success. It's all about consciously and constantly staying focused and keeping things in perspective and staying balanced.

Focus on the positive and not the negative, give all of your time and energy to the things you want to attract and accomplish in your life, think about what you want and not what you don't. Keep in perspective that where you are and what you're going through is never as bad as it seems and it's only temporary. Someone would be blessed to have the struggles you have. I once read a quote, "If we all put our problems in a pile with a group of strangers then we all would rush to pick our own back up," I love this quote and I think it's so true because it's all about perspective.

I'll say it again, there's nothing wrong with wanting more or to do better, it even says in the bible you should ask for what your heart desires and it shall be given if you believe. What I think there is something wrong with is complaining about what you already have and where you currently are in life. My question is why complain? There's absolutely nothing it can do for you or your situation, it won't get you out of where you are now and it won't help you get to where you want to go. Complaining is like going to the gym but not working out; it's a waste of time.

Complaining often turns small problems into bigger ones; if we would do less complaining about the problem and put more energy into finding a solution, then these little problems would not be such a big unnecessary stress on our lives. As cliché as it sounds, life is really 10% what happens to you and 90% of how you respond; there are thousands of stories of others who have been in worse situations than the one you're in and came out alright. These people don't look for the little excuses that would allow them to stay in the situation that they're in, they look for ways and reasons to get out.

We often blow little things out of proportion when things don't seem to go our way in life and what we fail to realize is that giving a small thing a big amount of energy will only have a negative effect on us. It's very difficult to complain about something while simultaneously trying to find a way to solve the problem. In life, we never stay in the same spot, we're either going forward or backward and our attitude on life will pretty much determine that. Our attitude is that little thing that make a big difference.

# CHOOSE TO THINK
# FOR YOURSELF

A second chance to view your life and how you used to live it and take it for granted, some people call it growth or maturity. To realize that you're not obligated to be permanently who you were yesterday or who you are today will empower you more than anything else in life. You are awakened to the ultimate power of choice. You have the power to change your life and your situation at any given moment. I'm not a fan of habits because they tend to cause you to think less, I like to consciously do everything on purpose with a purpose.

Now, obviously, some habits are good and some are bad, that goes without saying. The only thing worse than a habit, good or bad, is choosing not to think. I highly dislike when people say "I hate that I think too much". We all know that thinking of the wrong things can be bad and frustrating but that is not the same as thinking too much; I don't believe there is a such thing. My question is what's wrong with thinking? That's better than not thinking at all, if you don't consciously think for yourself then someone else will feed your subconscious and think for you.

Your thinking will be influenced more or less by the environment you're in and the people you're around, the media, what you listen to, and anything else that has access to your greatest gift; your mind. It's inevitable that to some degree we're all influenced by external things outside ourselves but when you never stop thinking and challenging things, you learn to evaluate and filter what you accept. I understand the importance of certain situations where being decisive quickly is far better than thinking to the point to where you delay making the decision itself; there's a time and place for that.

As a firefighter, we have very little time to think when we're going into a structure fire, you have to decide quickly and assess the risk and reward while sizing up the situation. We rely more so on our training than thinking in the heat of the battle and that's why training is so important for us. Life is not a game of checkers, it's chess; we must think through our plan so when we decide to act we can do less thinking and be more effective. Train your mind in the direction you want your body and life to go and it'll never steer you wrong. We focus so much on training our body physically before we master our mind, which naturally takes care of the body.

We must think before we act. We must know why we're taking the actions we're taking and be committed to that and the consequences that comes with it. Good habits may lead to good things but if you don't think things through and constantly revaluate your habits or why you created them, then it may lead you to a life that you don't want. It is possible to be successful at the wrong thing, something you don't truly desire. We see it all the time, parents forcing higher education on their kids or making them major in something that the kid has no interest in and that ultimately leads to resentment. This is why you must learn to think for yourself because it's the only way to end up healthy, wealthy, happy, and successful.

Everything is not for everyone, we all have to decide to live the life that's best for us, not what others think that's best for us. This is true with life in general; we must know what we want so we know what to look for and this enables us to ignore distractions, even the things that look similar to what we want. We must first learn to think on our own to arrive at such meticulous exactness.

I believe we fail to think for ourselves like we should because thinking takes more effort than being influenced. We would rather be spoon fed than to prepare the meal ourselves because it takes more time and effort. Think about why we still eat fast-food even though we know it's bad for us? It's always ready, it's fast, you don't have to think about getting the recipe from the grocery store, and last but not least, it's convenient with our hectic schedules. Being influenced by others and not thinking is the same situation. People preach (no pun intended) what they preach to others because that's what they believe, they've already thought about it and decided or it was put on them without them having to think for themselves. People who don't think would rather listen to someone else than to think for themselves and it's quite sad.

Thinking does not mean that you always disagree with someone, it just means you did your homework and you know why you agree or disagree. The mind is nothing more than a tool that needs to be constantly sharpened. It needs to be constantly sharpened because we should be constantly using it. People who don't use their minds and think on the regular just sort of go through life on auto-pilot and will end up doing what the masses do, which is usually not good. We outright own two things in our lives: our thinking and our time, everything else is suspect and not as important. Choosing your thoughts carefully and using your time wisely alone can get you to any level of success and happiness you're trying to reach.

# PRIVILEGE VERSUS POVERTY

When you have nothing you then realize that you are everything that you need. We always hear the stories about people literally starting from the bottom with nothing; financially, mentally, no support system, and no hope in anything for that matter. Somehow, they manage to rise from their situation and become an amazing success story that inspires the world. How does this happen? When you're not given anything to start out to work in your favor this forces you to use the most important resource that you have, which is yourself. People who don't have a foundation to start out with create and make a way if they're ambitious enough.

When you're backed into a corner and surrounded by the walls and struggles of everyday life, it's either going to make you or break you; there's no in between. We tend to want to rely on others before we rely on ourselves but what we fail to realize is that holding ourselves accountable is the key to a lasting success. I'm not saying we don't need help to get to where we're going but relying on others to help us does no good until we become our own number one person to depend on. God even gives us free will; he can have all the blessings aligned for us with all the open doors but if we never decide to walk through than none of it will matter.

This is the advantage and the power of having nothing, you quickly realize that your source of power was never in a thing that you have or don't have. You ever wonder why people who come from privilege end up not being successful like all of their family generations before them? Then someone from poverty who started with absolutely nothing becomes this great success story? You can inherit a lot of things, a family business, money, and anything else that would seem to put you at an advantage and set you up to be successful but you cannot inherit success or the drive it'll take to get there.

Having all of those things doesn't make you successful, most of the time it can even make it more difficult because they've never been in a position to have to rely on themselves for anything. This is why a lot of successful people started from humble beginnings, especially, a lot of your wealthy CEOs or people who start their own business or what not instead of working for others. They understand what it takes to depend first on yourself before asking anyone else for help. It's not necessary for people who grow up in privilege to be able to depend on themselves because all the resources are already set to be successful.

To what most of society defines as "success", privilege kids are already fortunately successful from the day they're born without ever having to do any work. They have financial freedom just because of their last name; some have a business passed down to them because of their mom and dad. I'm not saying this is a bad thing, just because two things correlate doesn't mean they cause one another, I'm just simply stating the reasons for the different types of drive for success that a person of privilege and poverty can have.

Someone in poverty has everything to gain while a kid in privilege may have everything to lose. You can let your children inherit your business (as you should) but you cannot make them inherit the drive that you had to build that business and maintain its success. They don't sell ambition, it's in you or it's not; if they did sell it, I'm sure the privileged would probably be the only ones able to afford it. That's not the case, thank God, and that is the secret to success; it's not where you come from in life, it's what you make of life.

This is what makes poverty a mindset; you have to believe and know you can do better before you can do better. If you're not somehow exposed to anything better, then you don't know that there is better or you know but you feel it can't happen for you because no one around you has done it. It usually takes for a family member, a coach, or a mentor to come into someone's life to speak life into them for them to realize that they can be just as successful as the next person if they put in the work. All it takes is a shift in thinking and then after that, literally, the sky is the limit.

I had recently done some research on what's called the "boiling frog syndrome" and I found it a very interesting study that helps me describe the point I'm trying to get across about being in an environment that can harm you and not allow you to break away and grow. They did a study back in the 1800's by putting a frog in a pot of water starting out at just room temperature and what they found out was that if they slowly increase the temperature of the water up to the point that it boils and kills the frog, the frog will never jump out if it's done gradually. The frog will eventually die not even giving itself a fighting a chance obviously not aware to the dangerous environment that it was in. When I thought about this it made me realize that there's no difference between the frog and humans that are in an environment that's harmful for us. If we knew better we would do better just like the study of the frog, you can't know what you don't know and this is what I like to call a silent killer.

When you don't know something is harmful to you and it just seems normal to you because everyone around you is doing it or that's what you're used to in your environment then it's hard to want to get out of your environment because you don't see any-thing wrong with it. In other words, your environment becomes a trap; you're not trapped because you "can't" leave, you're trapped because you don't know that you should leave. As I stated earlier, to live a better life one must be exposed to better things and see that opportunities do exist; the ignorance to the danger of an environ-ment is what keeps the rich people rich and the poor people poor.

The frog didn't notice the danger until it was too late, the dan-ger was so subtle that it couldn't tell the difference but the good news is that's not the case for people. We have the ability to think, step away, and fully-asses a situation for what it is and what we need to do to live the life we want to live. There's nothing or no one that can stop us from using our ability to think as well as our imagina-tion and will power to better ourselves.

We may not be able to control what we're born into and how we grow up but we can make changes if we don't like the way we're living at any time in our lives. Every day you wake up and take a breath it's never too late to want better for yourself. The frog has an excuse, we don't. We need to learn from the frog and get out of that pot of hot water before it burns us and we get used to the heat by thinking it's normal because we'll start to think we don't have a choice. We can jump out of that pot of water at any time when we work up the courage to do so because no one can control our thinking; they may build up a wall for you to never get out but there's always a way out, around, over, or under that wall. The wall is put up to discourage, the wall is not permanent, and as long as you control your mind then that physical and psychological wall doesn't stand a chance against a thinking man or woman who's on a mission for a better life than what was given to them.

# MISTAKES

The worse mistake you can make is being afraid to make one. The act, or lack of trying itself, prevents people from reaching greatness, success, and happiness more than failure ever could. We talk ourselves out of our dreams before we even try to pursue them. Our imagination tells us the exact life we want to live down to every detail in our minds but we tend to let our reality dominate our thoughts and control our actions. We let where we are now hold us hostage to a mediocre lifestyle. We talk ourselves into not feeling worthy of the life that we imagine in our minds. We let our sight, what we see now, negatively affect our vision on what we could become in the future and make a reality for the better.

What we fail to realize is that reality is not permanent, it's only permanent if you continue to do what you did in your past to get you to this reality today. It's never too late to start changing your lifestyle for the better to live the life you've always imagined. We often let the world and people around us dictate our lifestyle and the choices we make. We're often people pleasers and that's never healthy; we need to be what I like to call "me-pleasers". Being a me-pleaser doesn't mean you're selfish, it just means you've decided to do everything you have to do to live the life you've always wanted to live regardless of what anyone else thinks. Being a me-pleaser is ironically quite the opposite of being selfish.

When you become truly happy with what you're doing and living your purpose in life then people will be naturally drawn towards you for you to help them. Being happy and living your dream is contagious, people want to be around that because the average person is not truly happy with where they are in life and what they're doing. It inspires them when they see others in a position in life to where their work doesn't feel like work and it causes them to believe that if you can do it so can they. Being a me-pleaser is not just about you, it's about being an example for a cause that's greater than yourself.

To some degree some people will even come off as jealous or envy your way of life and those people aren't important. In all honesty, they don't hate you, they secretly admire you and the way you live. Hate isn't natural for us, hate is learned so we must not take our haters personally; don't give them your time or energy, just pray for them that they one day realize we're all in the same boat and we all can help each other to be healthy, happy, and successful.

Let's take a baby learning to walk for an example. They are not discouraged by failures or mistakes because they're by all rights me-pleasers. Their only goal is to learn to walk. No matter how many times they fall and fail, they want to walk because that's what they want. They can care less how many times they fall, who sees them fall, if they get hurt when they fall, or if their parents want to put them in a stroller because they're going in public. They're simply trying to satisfy their own need by any means. My question is why do we lose this type of mindset as we grow older?

Would you agree that everyone in the world would be healthier, happier, and more successful if we kept the same attitude we had while learning to walk? I sure do believe so and it's so ironic that the attitude that baby learning to walk has as being a me-pleaser is natural, that kid hasn't been on earth long enough for someone to instill that in them. As I stated earlier, it's natural for us to keep going after what we want despite failures and mistakes because God knows that it's necessary to have this mindset in order to succeed and be happy in this world. The Most High didn't design this world to not knock us down and stay there, but he designed us to keep getting back up no matter what.

The thing we do learn growing up from the outside world and even from our parents, family, spouses, and co-workers is that doubt, negativity, fear, and failure are bad things; to care what others think of us and putting limits on our dreams and lifestyles. We learn that money is more important than happiness and we think that money will make us happy. We learn that time is not the most important and precious commodity that there is so we learn to waste it without appreciating it. We also learn that "success" automatically equals happiness and we define success as what we accomplish versus who we are. We view success as what people think of us instead of what we think of ourselves and being me-pleasers.

This negative stuff that holds us back from happiness and success is learned, but there is a positive side to this negative. What's learned can always be unlearned, it's never too late like I said earlier. It may be more difficult to unlearn versus just learning but that's okay, difficult doesn't mean impossible. Unlearning is so hard because we are naturally creatures of habit and once something becomes a habit (whether it's right or wrong, bad or good), we no longer have to think as much as I've stated earlier. Once you do something for so long, you obviously tend to think it's right in order for you to keep doing it or you wouldn't keep doing it if you thought otherwise. Some people like to say people are stuck in their ways, all that stems from is thinking and doing something for so long that you see no logical reason to change nor do you care to look for one and this is the same concept. This, in itself, is what creates ignorance. (Ignorance - lack of knowledge.)

To unlearn, you have to constantly and consciously undo all the things you've done and thought that you wish to change; this is not an overnight process. Maturity, growth, and learning shouldn't have an age limit, this is why remaining humble enough to continue to learn is important for us to achieve greatness. We don't know everything and we never will so to become comfortable with only what we already know is the road to ignorance. This is what makes unlearning such a process in itself; to admit there's a better way to doing or thinking versus how you're used to and then to find a better way and then to actually change your ways can be a real challenge for us all.

I know from personal experience that changing a habit is not easy and it takes time. I have to constantly tell myself what I'm doing and why because I'm constantly fighting being comfortable and my old habits. Like I said, once we live a certain lifestyle and get comfortable with it, we see no desire to change it so we go on auto-pilot, if you will, with both our actions and thinking. When I want to change things, I have to write them down and read them daily to hold myself accountable until they become habits. I learned from studying successful people that I put sticky notes all around my house and write my goals all around the house so I see them on a regular basis to the point they become a part of me.

Another thing that I find really helpful is having accountability partners, these are people that you share your dreams and goals with and they know what you're trying to change so they hold you accountable to what you said you'll do. We must be careful and choose wisely with who we choose to share our dreams with because everyone is not for us but accountability partners are great to keep you on task. I can't speak for anyone else but when I have goals and set out to accomplish something I've never done, I have to consciously convince myself that I can and I will do it before it happens. I write down my goals in past tense as if I've already done them, this may sound overly meticulous but it's more powerful than you can imagine.

If you don't have faith and believe it before it happens then you'll never do it, you'll just continue to wait and hope for something better instead of claiming it. In order to be a me-pleaser you have to know you can do it or it'll never work. If a baby thought he/she would never walk then they wouldn't continue to try after they've fallen so many times. Having the vision, believing it, then working hard until it becomes a reality is pretty much the process to changing your reality to building a better future.

# THE GRASS IS NOT GREENER

It's much more difficult to hold someone down versus lifting someone up, yet we continue to try to hold each other down because we think someone is going to get an opportunity that should be ours. It's enough blessings to go around for everyone and I mean EVERYONE! It's hard to spot opportunities when you're focused on someone else's blessings. If you want someone else's blessings then you must also want their struggles as well, you don't get one without the other because they sure didn't.

Before any triumph, we must first go through adversity; there can't be a testimony if you're never tested. Nothing seems what the reality of it actually is from the outside looking in. We tend to have this fetish of wanting to be where others are without knowing where they've been. The main issue that this creates for us is that it creates an illusion as if their life is somehow better than our own. If you think someone's life is better than yours then you've lost sight in the value of you being you.

The power of advertising is more powerful than we realize because it presents the illusion that something we don't have is better than what we already have. Big businesses and companies realize this and that's why they spend billions of dollars on advertising. The power to influence you through the media, radio, music, internet, TV, billboards etc. is what pretty much runs the world today. They aim to influence your subconscious mind because your subconscious can be influenced without you even realizing it.

Advertising is powerful because it makes you forget that you actually do have a choice. They try to make you feel like you need what they're selling, like their grass is greener on the other side of the fence, meaning they'll only show you what they want you to see and they'll only tell you what they want you to know. I'm here to tell you that the grass is greener wherever you water and nurture it.

If you're not conscious enough to filter these things before they enter your subconscious then before you realize it, you'll be at McDonalds buying that new burger on that commercial even though you know it's not healthy or you'll be buying those new designer clothes that you know you cannot afford. You may have a quick pleasurable satisfaction from the perspective of your taste buds but in the future it may clog your arteries or that new outfit may put you deep in credit card debt so in other words, you'll always pay for it later. Everything has its price, success and failure, nothing is free so if you're looking at someone else's success or blessings you must be conscious enough to realize that they've paid for where they are at that present time.

Don't lie to yourself and downplay their hard work because you want to take short cuts, don't convince yourself that that's true. Just like you shouldn't let a commercial convince you that you need to go try this new unhealthy food or buy this expensive clothing or shoes to feel worthy. Knowing exactly who you are, what you want, and never settling for anything less than that is the best and only motivation. We must block out all other noise and distractions to be able to keep this focus. People who don't know what they want tend to be the easiest people to influence. When you don't know exactly what you want then your energy and concentration has no specific direction to work toward. If that's the case, then you'll just have interest in things that are presented to you by others and you won't be committed to a purpose.

The difference between commitment and interest is in the "why" you're doing something. If you don't know why it is you do what you do then when things get hard you're going to lose interest, quit, and move on to something else. There are a lot of people in this world who are interested in being healthy, happy, wealthy, and successful but they're not willing to commit and pay the price for it. They may think and tell you that they're committed to happiness and success but they have no idea.

To be committed to happiness and success you have to truly love yourself to be able to commit to keeping and sustaining happiness and success; this goes for commitment towards anything. All of these things start from within, there is no greater success in life than being unreasonably happy about you and your life. It's not what you do but it's how you feel about what you do; it's not about what you receive but it's about what you give, to yourself and others. It's not about accomplishing things but it's about living a life of value and significance to make your life and others better.

Everything you set out to do in life will have a journey because all great things take time. There are no shortcuts to any journey worth traveling, it's the road less traveled but there are controllable factors that will determine the quality of every second of those journeys. We can't decide how long the journey is going to be, but we can decide how much fun it's going to be. We can't decide how many hurdles we're going to run into on the journey but we can work on our hurdle form to use the roadblocks as motivation instead of becoming discouraged and use each set back as stepping stones to become better and stronger.

# MY GOD AND MY DOORS

People always say "if it's meant to be it will be" and I think that statement is overused and often misunderstood. No matter what blessing God puts in front of us or what door he opens, we have the free will to accept the blessing or not for whatever reason. It might be that we don't believe we're good enough, we're full of doubt, fear, or we think the opportunity will not be there forever or my favorite, if it's meant to be it will be. The thing is if we decide not to go through those doors God opens for us, for whatever reason, and just wait until we feel we're ready then we can miss out on our blessings because when God closes the door it's all over. You may tell yourself it wasn't meant to be but you really know deep down inside you messed up your blessing; you literally missed out on that opportunity and the least you can do is be honest with yourself.

Whether it's a career choice or choice to be with a significant other, if you wait too long and expect that opportunity or person to wait on you forever then you're literally digging yourself in a hole to miss your blessing. No person, nor any situation, stays the same over time, the window will eventually close on any opportunity. God will not place a blessing in front of you if he felt you couldn't handle it, but when it boils down to it, the main person that has to believe that is YOU. Again, we have the free will to accept our blessings or not and also our choice to give God the credit for it or not.

We often make it seem like we don't have free will. I read a quote before that said, "Opportunity knocks once, maybe twice if you're lucky but temptation leans on the doorbell." I believe this to be very true in life. I think it's very simple, God is the maker of the opportunities, blessings, and open doors, those are his blessings, favor and gifts to us. For example, a chance to have your dream career whether it's the NBA, become an actor, artist, entrepreneur, architect, model, doctor, dentist etc. but the temptations and worldly things get in your head to distract you and say "what if" causing you to keep from pursuing it; that's our own free will of choice.

I can only speak for me but I cannot live without trying for something that I really want to at least see how it'll work out. When you do decide to take a leap of faith and go through the door that God opened specifically for you not knowing what's on the other side, that's when you can say "if it's meant to be it will be". It shows that you are trying; you got out of your comfort zone and decided to trust in God that if you take a step he'll show you the rest of the way.

Not knowing if that career, dream, or relationship will work scares everyone, not just you but also the ones who don't let that fear overcome their faith. Using the free will that God gave you shows that you're willing to take the chance to have a fulfilling life and many more blessings to come with that courage. The thing about faith is that it's not easy, it cannot be explained or disproven, it's not based on emotion, logic, or rational thinking and your environment, teachers, family, and friends will literally discourage you from it if you let them. I believe the unknown is the thing most feared by people, sad to say it should be God but it's not. Us not knowing doesn't just cause us to just live in fear but it causes us to have fear of making a mistake and not acting on things because of that fear, which is far worse.

The bible has many definitions for faith but the most popular one is probably (Hebrews 11) "Faith is the substance of things hoped for and the evidence of things not seen." To put in my own words, faith is knowing the unknown. Now you may be thinking how can you know the unknown? My answer is the closer you become to God, listen to his voice inside of you, and believe he's bigger than any obstacle life can throw at you then the more of the unknown you will know and he will reveal to you. By building a relationship with the Most High you will learn not to lean on your own understanding. Faith really cannot be explained but you will know when you have it and it's very easy to see if someone else has it even if you don't.

We like for things to be certain and this is what contributes to our faith being so little because we don't like risk. We fear going out on a limb even if it does have the possibility of making our lives better. We are programmed to think about what can go wrong versus what can go right; it's not about being naive and not realizing things can go wrong but if you want it bad enough, you'll persist and learn something in every temporary defeat to get you closer to your success. This is why people live so small because we want people to give us this if we do that, we lack the spirit of risking more to become more. What we will fail to realize in this is that faith is not learning to fly then jumping, but it's jumping then learning to fly.

"Trust in The Lord with all your heart, and lean not on your own understanding; in all your ways acknowledge him, and he shall direct your paths. Do not be wise in your own eyes." (Proverbs 3:5-7) For a long time I didn't really understand this scripture the way I should've until I began to write this chapter for this book. One day, I was reading my bible in the morning and this scripture jumped out at me and the Holy Spirit spoke to me and gave me a revelation. I used to think that not leaning on my own understanding was to somehow say I wasn't competent enough to make my own decisions but as I grew, I realized that this is not what this scripture was about. This scripture is to help protect us from ourselves when we are hesitant to go through doors that God has opened.

I know from personal experience that I tend to procrastinate when I don't have everything figured out to my understanding to how it's going to work out. That is why this scripture is for people like me but God is telling us in this word that we don't need to have it all figured out from a logical standpoint to take action. He's telling us that if we go toward that door he has opened without understanding everything, he then says "he shall direct our paths". He said "do not be wise in your own eyes" meaning don't think that you're smart enough to figure out how God's promise for your life will unfold just believe and have faith that the promise will be delivered. Once you make the decision to go after your heart's desires then you have to tell God that's what you want and take action, he'll figure out the rest like he said he would. We must not let our understanding or lack thereof hold us back any longer because if we understood God's big plans and blessings for our lives there would be no need for the Most High.

There is no such thing as bad timing or a wrong door or blessing being presented in our lives. We may not always get what we want when we want it but if we continue to persist and give everything we have, then and only then, can we truly understand God's timing is always perfect. It's hard to understand someone if you don't truly know them. At some point we've all questioned why do bad things happen to good people, but that's the wrong question and perspective if you want to live a life of happiness. Difficult or bad things happen to strong people who can handle it, if it was too much to handle then God wouldn't have allowed the situation to become a reality.

With every risk we take there will be adversity but every time we get knocked down, there's a lesson in it to make us realize that we're stronger than we actually thought. We fail to realize that it's often and only these chain of "bad things" that happen to us that are the exact things we needed to bring out the best in us. Every situation is literally what you think and make of it; you can either "choose" to complain about it and say how it holds you back or use a hard time as a stepping stone to build strength and become better and go further in life.

The free will we have to choose to define whatever we will often backfires against our own power we have to be used in a positive way. We get caught up in what we see, learn, and take from others then we make it our own reality. We forget there's only two different ways to learn from other people's lives: what to do and what not to do. We must remember that we can choose to exercise what not to do while observing and being around others. We give up our power of independent thinking. No one that's lived before you or will live after you is smarter or better than you are and you aren't superior to them either.

There's no rule that says you have to do or live your life based on what someone else has or hasn't done, I'm talking about your parents, peers, family, friends, co-workers, or anyone else; they don't define you or your future. You have the power to create a new set of rules to live by to enjoy a better lifestyle. The power of defining what happens to us and how we react to it after we take a leap of faith is the DNA of our attitude, which will eventually motivate our actions or discourage us.

# FAITH VERSUS BEING POSITIVE

*"For myself, I am an optimist - it does not seem to be much use in being anything else."*

*- Winston Churchill*

I'm an optimist by nature but my faith is on purpose. I'm naturally a positive person because it's just a part of my personality but your personality isn't always congruent with reality. Personality has a lot to do with how you feel and how you tend to think, it's more emotional than factual. Faith is more of a reality that's yet to be proven, it's something in your heart that you know that's already going to be but time just hasn't caught up to the blessing in real time yet. A positive attitude or being an optimist is a great thing, it's definitely healthy and better than being negative all the time because that will get you nowhere. Being an optimist can more so point you in the right direction but one must have faith in order to know what the destination is in order to execute and get the results that you want. For this, faith is necessary and more important than just being positive.

It's not what you do but it's how you do it, why you do it, and does it help others by what you get out of it. If you have faith in something, your joy beforehand is no different than when you actually get there because you already knew based on your faith what that was and what it was going to be before it actually happened. Being positive can and will have you psyched up temporarily but, eventually, you will have negative thoughts. You can compare it to people making the same New Year's resolutions to go to the gym. While making the resolution you feel good and positive about it but for most people, once that feeling goes away so does them working out. That's when your faith is tested.

One cannot achieve greatness on positivity alone because no matter what, everything in life isn't always positive or perfect. Things will happen to you in life that will seem to suck the life out of you, let alone the positivity. Studies show that on average we think about 60,000 thoughts a day, somewhere in there will be some negative thoughts and that's inevitable. That doesn't mean you shouldn't consciously try to feed your mind as much positivity as possible. You definitely want the positive to outweigh the negative as much as you can.

We don't want to confuse progress with perfection because progress is realistic and should be the goal, while perfection doesn't exist in anyone or anything except God. Just like being positive all the time is not realistic but having the faith that the negative can and will have a purpose to be used for something to learn from and make us better is more realistic. Faith gives you a purpose or a "why" to keep going even when things aren't perfect, it's something so much bigger than the circumstance. A positive attitude alone doesn't carry that much power because it's not that deep. It may cause you to get through a day with a smile on your face but faith will cause you to have a great purposeful life, which I hope is everyone's ultimate goal.

Optimism controls more of the mind and feelings but faith comes from the core; the heart and soul of who you truly are and why you do what you do. This is the single most important thing for a person, what he/she lives for and what drives them when they wake up every single day and how much faith they have in it.

# GOD'S PLAN

What does it mean to really trust in God's plan? I often have conversations with friends and family about believing in God's plan and where the fine line is between working your plan and submitting to The Lord's will. Our heart's desires and his will for our lives often seem to conflict from a logical standpoint. I know from personal experience that this has happened on more than one occasion and for me, there's no greater stress than not knowing when to keep going or move on.

With all that we can imagine to desire, it's very hard to believe from a limited human's view and rationale that God can have something in store for us that's better. What can be better than all you can imagine? God's plan for your life is the only answer. I think the biggest misconception is just because God's plan is better than ours does not make our plans and our desires any less important than his; they actually coincide with one another. In fact, our heart's desires and plans are vital to go after and achieve in order to discover God's true will for our lives.

Nothing is concrete about this because everyone's personal situation and relationship with God is different. I truly believe discovering God's will for our life is important for two reasons: 1. The plan we have will not go exactly how we planned to get there even if the destinations stay the same. 2. The destination for God's will in your life may be different than yours but you do have the free will to accept that or not. Whatever decision you make you are not free from the consequences that comes with the choices that you've made.

You may even achieve a level of "success" doing things your way but there will always be a void left unfulfilled in your life if you don't do it God's way. This is present every day in our society from people who have achieved great success and have more money, fame, and everything else they ever could but end up killing themselves or strung out on drugs. This is not saying success has caused that but my point is that success and achievements alone are not enough to keep them happy.

As I've stated earlier on in this book if we knew better we would do better so how can we possibly pursue a plan that doesn't exist for us? When we know God, we will do better is a more accurate statement for the point I'm trying to get across. Knowing God is what will allow you to make the decision to keep pursuing that desire or move on to something bigger (God's plan) and better with confidence and no regrets. Regret is far worse than any failure or temporary defeat ever will be. You can learn from failures and mistakes in life but regret is what kills people from the inside out making it far worse than a physical death. People who live with major regrets are walking around in life dead on the inside, this hurts and will make you a miserable person.

These people never pursued their heart's desires to see what would or could happen, their fear of failure outweighed their faith for a possibility of success. The heart is the body's lifeline and it must be working in order for us to live. The heart pumps out oxygenated blood via arteries to feed the body's organs and it receives that same blood back via veins again but it's deoxygenated and the process starts over.

In our heart also lives God and our true desires or our purpose in life. If you don't attempt to live these desires then they will lay in your heart, become dormant, and it will not be a good feeling. You will, without even realizing it, become a negative person who'll discourage others from their dreams and aspirations and no one will want to be around you. You'll start to hate what you do for a living because your heart aches and longs daily for it's true desire but you ignore it and keep playing it safe. You'll subconsciously become jealous and envious of others who are living out their true desires. We fail to realize that if we pursue these desires then it's always a win/win situation; either you'll get what you desire or the Most High will reveal something better.

Facing the fear of failure will empower you to accomplish anything in life and in the near future and the process will have less power over you because you've been there before. Fear only has power as long as we give it the power. You can and will fail eventually at something in life (unless you choose not to do anything and that's worse than failing); if you don't pursue what you want then you'll fail at something you don't want so common sense says you might as well give your true desires a shot. Success isn't the absence of failure but failure has the presence of quitting and that's the only difference. The only way to become one with God is to make what's in your heart a reality. The only reason I say that is because I truly believe that God is the one who put it in your heart in the first place.

God wrote the blueprint for each and every one of our lives long before we got here and the only way to live and be that light that he put into us is to become one with him. There's no better way to learn and exercise your strengths than to build a relationship with the one who gave them to you. Our future to God is the past to him so knowing him is like literally knowing the future. I'll put it to you like this, that burning desire in your heart that never goes away for you to become that exact thing and person is your future.

Most of us know what we were born to do or at least know the direction we need to go but the problem is the fear of attempting to live that life and never making it. What we fail to realize is that on the journey to that desire, God will reveal everything we need to get to the appropriate next step. We're so worried about steps C - Z but we actually haven't even taken action to go from step A to B. This is the fine line and importance between long and short-term goals; they're both necessary but the timing is vital and will make or break your success. Once we take that first step from A to B, God will reveal what's necessary for the next steps at that appropriate time and so on.

If we really sit back and think about it, why would God reveal to us every single step we need to take to get to our destination at one time? That would literally overwhelm us. Just thinking about your life and how you realize you have so much to do in a day but not enough time will literally cause us to get frustrated until we take a deep breath and make ourselves focus on one thing at a time because that's the best way to get things done. Like Dr. Martin Luther King Jr. said, "Faith is taking the next step without seeing the whole staircase." He hit the nail right on the head with that quote. The whole staircase will never be revealed to us so if that's what we're waiting on then we'll be waiting forever and never start. This is what some of our lives are like, we're waiting on perfect timing to see the entire plan before we take action.

We want things guaranteed before we put forth our efforts. This violates every natural law in life; nothing is guaranteed except death and paying taxes. We want to see what we will reap before we sow it. Why do we seek exceptions to the rules when it comes to taking a chance to living out our dreams? It's because of the lack of faith and the presence of fear. We all have both fear and faith within us but the one we feed more is the one that will persist and take up most of the space in our hearts causing us to live accordingly.

Just like the heart pumps out blood, we must live out our dreams, give our blessings out, and not hold them within. You have to let things go to grow and prosper to see if they'll become all they can be and come back; hoarding anything is never healthy. Just think, if the heart feared that the blood it pumped out to feed the body's vital organs would never come back to feed the heart again and start the cycle over. If that was the case and the heart decided to hold on to the blood out of that fear, then the heart would literally fill up with blood and drown itself. This is what happens when we don't pursue our heart's desires; we're alive on the outside but dead on the inside because we're holding things in that need to be lived out and given to the rest of the world. There's no worse way to die than to die with dreams inside.

"The wealthiest place on earth is the graveyard, because so many people die with books, ideas, inventions, and all of their dreams inside without living them." Don't become a part of that saying, take a chance to live your dreams and God's will will guide you to exactly where you need to be. Dreams and desires aren't meant to stay in that state as only dreams, they're meant to be manifested into reality.

# CONCLUSION

I really pray that after reading this book you've learned more about yourself than you've learned about me. I'm a work in progress so I can only speak on the little that I know of this world that I've experienced thus far. I'm no expert by any means in this thing called life because the only thing I know for sure is that I don't know much. My stories and testimonies are just a reflection of how great our God is and how he continues to shower me with blessings and favor even though I fall short of righteousness daily. All the glory, praise, and everything that I wrote in this book is thanks to God. I've been blessed to use my experiences to inspire others with my gift to be able speak and write to relate to people and bring them into my world so they can see that they are not alone and that they can do anything they put their minds to.

As I stated in the beginning, this book is not a "key" or "guide" to happiness and success but it's more of a reality that you have to know who you are before you can achieve anything remotely close to happiness. You must have a purpose that's bigger than you to become all that you can be; we must have a specific and meaningful why for what we do. You can't take accomplishments, money, success, or anything else with you when you die, but you can leave behind a legacy that will help other generations and live on forever. We must become more so we can give more because love and giving are the only things that truly last. People will never forget how you loved them or what you gave them, I'm not talking about material things because the best gift you can give someone is the gift God put in you.

Happiness and success is something we have to decide upon every single day that we wake up, it's never automatic. We must decide consciously that we're going to focus more on our blessings rather than our problems. We don't ignore our problems but we indeed must handle them and find solutions. We must not dwell too much and stress over them because it does us no good, it's a waste of time and life is too short.

God's plan for our life exceeds anything of our own thinking ability so we must not think realistically in order to reach our full-potential. We must always shine our light from within so there can be less darkness in the world; don't dim your light because some-one else isn't using theirs. There is nothing this world can offer you that's not already in you, you don't need to chase anything or anyone in this world because God is in you and you can attract everything that your heart desires. If you will just take a leap of faith and believe that every day may not be perfect but they all have a purpose and each day has a blessing even when it doesn't feel like it, then you will live truly fulfilled. Believe that we always have a choice to be happy or miserable, as well as becoming a failure or a success.

## *Favorite Quotes And Scriptures*

Phil 4:13 – "I can do all things through Christ who strengthens me."

Hebrews 11 – "Faith is the substance of things hoped for and the evidence of things not seen."

Joshua 1:9 – "I will be strong and courageous. I will not be terrified, or discouraged; for the Lord my God is with me wherever I go."

"People are as happy as they make their mind up to be"

- Abraham Lincoln

"Information changes situations, knowledge is the new money."

- Dr. Eric Thomas

"Learn as if you will live forever but live as if you will die tomorrow."

- Gandhi

"You can do anything you put your mind to"

- My Mother (Marian Blackshear)

"It's a great day to have a great day."

- Peris DeVohn

"The power to think as you wish to think is the only power over which you have absolute control, rather it's positive or negative."

- Napoleon Hill

"I'm confessing that my blessings are greater than my problems therefore I have no right to complain."

- Peris DeVohn

"Your dreams are never too big, your thinking is just too small, you can do it."

- Peris DeVohn

"There are essentially two things that will make you wiser, the books you read and the people you meet."

- Charles "Tremendous" Jones

"If you cannot be positive, then at least be quiet."

- Joel Osteen

"You may not be able to control every situation and its outcome, but you can control your attitude and how you deal with it."

- Author Unknown

# ACKNOWLEDGEMENTS

First and foremost I'd like to thank My Lord and Savior Jesus Christ

My hero and my mother, Marian Blackshear, My entire family, The Blackshears' too many to name you all. Donovan Potter, Dre Rudolph, Morris Council, Shalise Lugo, David Springs, Ashley Yancey, Oli Shaheer, Jamie Poston, Shea/Mike Menchaca, Diamond Cole, Mrs. Peters, Rick Rios, Jason Moss, The Rouleau family, Joe Boyle, Ed Hardy, Matt Skotynsky, LaKata, George Findley, Rashad Cobham, Rose Bush, Ms. Diana Patton, Jessica Daniels, Jessica Vazquez, Amerah Archer, Gabby Hill, Melondy Anderson, Jasmine White, Scott, Amanti, Alpha Phi Alpha Inc, special thanks to the Delta Upsilon Chapter, Last but not least my Lady Monika Lignae you're my best blessing yet, and anyone else that has ever supported me, believed in me, read my blogs, or watched my youTube videos. From the bottom of my heart I say thank you, it was a team effort.

Made in the USA
San Bernardino, CA
04 April 2018